FOLLOWING GOD
THROUGH THE BIBLE
BIBLE STUDY

An informative **6 WEEK BIBLE STUDY** of life principles for today, to guide the church and the Christian's walk.

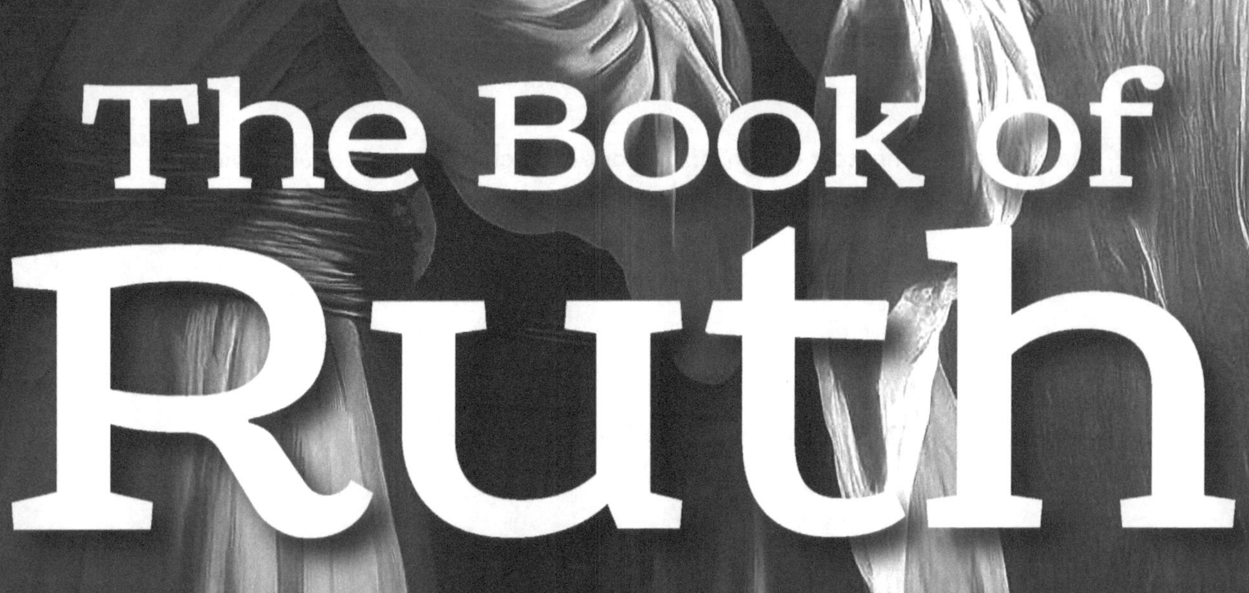

# The Book of Ruth

# Following God

## THE BOOK OF RUTH



Published by AMG Publishers. 

ISBN 13: 978-1-61715-626-7



Manuscript editing, text design, and layout by Rick Steele Editorial Services
http://steeleeditorialservices.myportfolio.com

Cover illustration by Daryle Beam/Bright Boy Design

*Printed in the United States of America*

***The Book of Ruth* is dedicated to . . .**

my constant, lovingly supportive husband, Stan;

our precious children and their dear spouses:

Lindsey, Jenna and Tyler, Maegan Ruth and Zachary, and Tyler and Cassie;

and to my precious little lambs:

Andrew, Luke, MollyKate, Caleb, Lucie, Hazel, and soon to arrive, unnamed granddaughter;

In each of you, I visibly see the providential kindness of our God in my life daily.

I love you all more than words!

# Acknowledgments

I would gratefully like to acknowledge . . .

- The late theologian Spiros Zodhiates, whose scholarly work and faithful ministry I am eternally indebted to.
- AMG Publishers, specifically Amanda Jenkins and my editor, Rick Steele, whose work is impeccable and whose ministry is necessary and encouraging.
- Transforming the Heart Ministry Team: Gigi Wootten, whose encouragement and prayer ministry, along with Sarah Coles, whose gift of administration are the backbone of the ministry. Co-laboring with you both is an honor, joy, and blessing.
- Transforming the Heart Ministry Board Members, whose loving and kind support make co-laboring for the gospel not only possible but a privilege and great joy: Stan Clark, Greg Wootten, John Taylor, Tyler Clark, Lindsey Clark, Maegan Pittinger, Julie O'Bryan, Megan Prewitt, and Michelle Burton.
- And most of all, my highest acknowledgment to my "compassionate and gracious, slow to anger, and abounding in lovingkindness and truth" LORD, GOD: Precious Father, Son, and Holy Spirit—to God be the glory forever and ever, Amen. Your gracious and loving providence has been so very kind!

## Mendy Clark

MENDY CLARK (DEd Min, Southwestern Baptist Theological Seminary) is a Bible teacher, author, retreat speaker, educator and discipler of women. She is the founder, executive officer, and lead teacher of Transforming the Heart Ministries. Transforming the Heart is a ministry dedicated to making disciples by equipping and training them using the biblical framework established in the all-sufficient Word of God.

# INTRODUCTION LESSON

## Welcome to the study of the Book of Ruth!

You hold in your hands a precious redemptive story of our gracious Lord, who is compassionate and gracious, slow to anger, and abounding in lovingkindness and truth" (Ex. 34:6).

It's the story of one obscure ordinary Jewish family living during some very dark and oppressive years in Israel's history. It's a story of faith tested, the subtlety of sin, and the sometimes "hard" providence of God as in mercy, He redemptively disciplines His children to bring them back to Himself.

More importantly, it resides within a much bigger story, His story—which makes it uniquely beautiful.

But before we dive into the story, we need to lay some fundamental foundations for good Bible study.

Are you ready to get started?

**A General Overview**

First, the Bible is a collection of sixty-six (39 Old Testament, 27 New Testament) books inspired by God with one unified story. Although it is one big story, not all books within the Bible are written in narrative (story) form. If you were to break down the entire Bible into three major literary styles, you would discover that almost half of the Bible is narrative (story), and one-third is poetry, such as the songs, wisdom writings, and the prophets. The rest is written in prose discourse, which views the Scripture logically and sequentially, requiring reasoning, such as the Law, its various speeches, and letters.

Similarly, when considering a narrative (or any book of the Bible), it is also necessary to consider the historical context. The events in each story are real-life events in time and space in history, and each story fits into the broader historical context of the entire Bible.

Theologians refer to this approach of study as biblical theology. Biblical theology is "the discipline of learning how to read the Bible as one story by one divine author that culminates in the person and work of Christ so that every part of Scripture is understood in relation to Christ."

In their book *Christ from Beginning to End*, authors Trent Hunter and Steven Wellum give three insightful ways to think through any given text, namely:

**Close Context**—The reader is encouraged to "Look down at the page and seek to understand the words in their immediate context," taking into account the words' divine inspiration and human character.

**Continuing Context**—Look back in the story to read a passage according to the Bible's "unfolding drama." The continuing context considers where the words are in relation to what has come before them in the unfolding story.

**Complete/Canonical Context**—We should look ahead in the story even when we read earlier parts before the coming of Jesus because the Bible is ultimately centered on Jesus Christ. The complete context considers the Bible's message centered in Christ and brought to bear on our lives.

You see, when reading any book of the Bible, we should look ahead for the One in whom the entire Bible is centered: our Lord and Savior, Jesus Christ. In fact, a careful observation and study will reveal that all sixty-six books point to Him.

Read Luke 24: 44–47 and record what Jesus said about the Old Testament writers and Scriptures.

---

---

Similarly, this was also the apostle's approach; for example, see Paul in Acts 17:1–3; 28:23–24, 30–31; 1 Corinthians 15:3–5; and Peter in 1 Peter 1:10–12. Even Apollos pointed to Christ from the Old Testament in Acts 18:24–28.

Doesn't it just make sense that if Jesus and His disciples viewed the Bible through this lens, shouldn't we?

In summary, the Old Testament writers looked forward to Christ in anticipation and hope, and the New Testament writers looked backward at Him in praise and gratitude. Jesus Christ is the central message of the entire Book. We must consistently read each Book, asking the Spirit to open our eyes to see a real and personal God sovereign over His work of creation and redemption. And if you love a good love story, you will find within the pages of your Bible the most remarkable love story ever told between the Creator and His creation.

As we study, be careful not to fall into the trap that the Bible is a story primarily about humanity. Whenever we make the Bible people-centered rather than God-centered, we become guilty of mishandling the Word of truth. Therefore, as careful Bible students, let us begin our study with the understanding that the Bible is God's revelation about Himself, and His purposeful plan in creation and redemption is the primary focus. Anything less can lead to error. With these things in mind, let's look at the Book of Ruth.

## THE BOOK OF RUTH

As we begin our study of the Book of Ruth, we will carefully watch its "Close, Continuing, and Complete" context woven throughout the story. We will focus on the people, places (including time), and events (the plot and the plot conflict) while also considering the time the story took place in history. While reading, we must remember that because there is ultimately a Divine Narrator, the words chosen and the sequence or order of events matter as the story unfolds. None of His words are random.

In this introduction lesson, our main objective is to familiarize ourselves with the book. We will read the entire story and make note of the specific people, places, and events within the narrative.

Take your time as you read. Consider dividing your days into a chapter per day. Feel free to go at your own pace because another foundational truth is never to read your Bible in a hurry!

In the next lesson, we will consider the first sentence of the book more closely. In it, you will discover the framework and backdrop of the entire book, which will prove necessary to understand how Ruth's "close context" relates to the "continuing and complete context" in Scripture. In doing so, we will make room for how the elements within the story can speak into our lives today without compromising the integrity of the context in which they were written.

Let's start by observing the entire book from a thirty-thousand-foot view.

Read the entire book in one setting and jot down your observations in the spaces provided. The introduction lesson is not the time to make interpretations or applications. It's simply an opportunity to read and familiarize yourself with the story.

Remember to begin your time of study daily in prayer because it takes God to understand God.

The people:

The places mentioned:

The main events:

2. Now, let's focus our attention on the first sentence in the book of Ruth, for it is full of Divine and purposeful meaning. Do you see three distinct phrases in verse 1? Record them in the order they appear.

   a. ______________________________

   b. ______________________________

   c. ______________________________

You might wonder, "Why have we started the study of Ruth in this way?" Do you see that the answer is that the text has driven it? Be encouraged! That's good Bible study! What does the text say, versus what do you think?

You will see, in the next lesson, how each phrase in Ruth 1:1 is distinctly separate and necessary to understand the book of Ruth and where it fits in the counsel of God's Word. Therefore, to accurately handle the book of Ruth, we will closely examine all three parts by looking back at the "continuing context" from which the story of Ruth begins. Until the next lesson, feel free to re-read this beautiful story of God's redeeming grace.

**Final Note:** To be able to fill in all blanks in this workbook, you will need access to the New American Standard Bible (1995 edition).

Mendy Clark

# CONTENTS

# Lesson 1

## The Providence of God: His Work in Redemption

Having been introduced to the Book of Ruth, we will look at the three phrases in Ruth 1:1. You might be thinking, "How can an entire lesson be devoted to one sentence?" But by the time we finish this lesson, you will see why. I purposely haven't divided the lesson into days, so that you can spend as much time as you need on each section. Are you ready to begin?

Before we dive into the text, we need to lay a little groundwork on how to interpret the Hebrew narrative. Therefore, we must start by addressing two interconnecting concepts: repetition and the "split-screen technique."

So often used in a biblical narrative, repetition is necessary for the sake of emphasis. By repeating people, places, and events, the narrator wants the reader to take notice and to be alert. In other words, there is something the reader must see to truly understand and correctly interpret the story's meaning and the things hidden within it—in essence, the story within the story.

Alongside repetition, pastor, author, and theologian Sinclair Ferguson refers to the "split screen technique." To explain this, I gratefully defer to Dr. Ferguson, who states,

> *In order to give us a sense of how God effects His providential purposes, Bible narratives sometimes use the literary equivalent of a movie maker's or television director's 'split screen' technique. They do with words what modern technology can do visually—splitting the screen so that we have two different perspectives simultaneously or can compare two different actions or events and relate them to each other. If you read Scripture narrative with that 'technique' In mind, you will notice how often Bible writers use it; not to make a sporting occasion appear more exciting and dramatic, but to give us an important insight into the nature of God's working.*[1]

In terms of its effectiveness, Ferguson explains, "When this split-screen technique is used, we are being encouraged to read the narrative from two different points of view; the human and the divine, the 'accidents' of history and *the activity of God's sovereignty* (emphasis added)."[2]

In summary, Ferguson is describing two perspectives necessary for proper interpretation: **1)** man's view of what he knows and sees, which, as you know, is partial, biased, and can be skewed, and **2)** God's perspective, which comes from total and complete knowledge (omniscience) that is just and entirely true. Both perspectives are happening simultaneously in any given biblical narrative. You will want to watch for both as we begin the story.

---

1 Sinclair Ferguson, *Faithful God: An Exposition of The Book of Ruth,* (Wales, UK: Bryntirion Press, 2005), pp. 52-53.
2 *Ibid.*, 53.

Do you see it?

On the left side, we have the Creator's perspective. On the right, Creation's perspective, wherein people make choices based upon what they see and understand.

Ultimately, the will of the One who is sovereign over all creation will providentially prevail!

With these things in mind, let's consider the first phrase, "Now it came about...," which begs the question, "Does anything in Scripture just simply 'come about'?" In short, the answer is "No." Nothing in Scripture or the world is merely coincidental or left to fate. Therefore, this little phrase should cause us to pause.

Because the Divine Author and Narrator chose to begin with these words, we must factor in another beginning from which every story in history originates—from eternity past.

So, let's begin by stating the obvious—the story from eternity past is much more complex. In fact, it is incomprehensible and cannot be seen apart from what God has chosen to reveal.

1. Begin by reading Deuteronomy 29:29 and answer the following questions:

    a. Record the two distinct categories: ______________ and _______________

    b. Who alone knows the secret things? _____________________

    c. To whom do the things revealed belong? ________________________________

    d. For what purpose did He choose to reveal these things? _____________________

As stated, the "secret things" can only be understood by God. Thankfully, He has chosen to reveal some things to us. The word "reveal" means to unveil.

In fact, one way He has chosen to reveal Himself progressively in Scripture is through His names, which unveil His divine nature, character, and attributes as God. Another way He reveals Himself is through His works. His names and His works are interconnected.

You will find both His names and works intricately interwoven throughout the Bible; some of the time, it will be hidden within the text. Moreover, it will never be fully seen or understood by human intellect because it's the story that originates in the sovereign and eternal counsel of the Godhead—The Father, The Son, and The Holy Spirit.

Think of it this way:

| **Who God Is** | **What God Is Doing** |
|---|---|
| **Elohim (GOD)** | Creative Work (Gen. 1:1) [Creator of all things heavenly and earthly] |
| **Yahweh (LORD)** | Redemptive Work (Gen. 2:4; Ex. 3:14–15). |

If you took a closer look at these two names, you would discover how each name of God corresponds with those created in His image. For example, Elohim describes His relationship with all humanity, while Yahweh, His covenant name, describes His relationship with those who are His children. Theologians define the first as general revelation and the second as special revelation.

General revelation is visible in His creation (Rom. 1:20) and the fact that every man has been given a conscience

(Rom. 1:19). In other words, there is an outside witness (Creation) and an inside witness (the human conscience) declaring that there is a God! Special revelation is seen in His Son and in His Word (Jn. 1:1; Heb. 1:1–2; Psalm 19:7–11; Heb. 4:12; and Rom. 10:17, to name only a few).

Furthermore, we have a God who speaks, and because He has chosen to reveal Himself through His Word, we must establish a working definition for biblical terms and concepts the Bible uses to demonstrate the truths of His Person and work (both creative and redemptive), starting with words such as sovereignty, providence, and the eternal counsel of God.

These words are necessary to define so we can attempt to understand what was "from before the foundation of the world." Phrases like "In the beginning, God created (Gen. 1:1), and "In the beginning was the Word and the Word was with God, and the Word was God...." (Jn. 1:1), help us begin to grasp the bigger story. That said, we should start with the term you are probably most familiar, His sovereignty.

**I. Sovereignty**

Let's start with the easiest way to remember the definition and look closely at the word as it appears. Do you see two words within the term that make up the definition?

________________ ________________

Can you see the words "reign" and "over"? If so, then this definition begs the question, "Reigns over what and who?" To answer this question, let's turn to the Scriptures.

Look at the following cross-references to verify and establish a biblical definition. By each reference, record what you see concerning the sovereignty of God both in His creative and redemptive work.

**Sovereignty: In His Creative Work**

a. Genesis 1:1 – What, how, and when did He create?

Did you notice His name, God (Elohim)? Did you see it revealed in reference to His work of creation, as He spoke the heavens and earth into existence before anything was created? Can you see that as the Creator of all things (heavens and earth), He is positionally over all things?

**Sovereignty: In His Redemptive Work**

b. Record His sovereign work in redemption (salvation). List the facts involved as He sovereignly saves His people. Read Exodus 3:7–15 and answer the following questions:

1) What did the LORD say in verse 7?

i. I have ____________ the _______________ of My people in Egypt,

ii. I have given ________________ to their ___________

iii. I am aware of their _________________________

2) What is the LORD doing in verse 8a? "I have __________ ____________ to ______________ them from the power of the Egyptians, and to bring them __________ from that land to a

_______________ and spacious land..."

Do you see the LORD'S sovereignty in salvation?

3) Moses inquires when the Israelites ask, "What is His name?" (v. 13); How does the LORD answer (v. 14)? ___________________________________

4) What does the LORD tell us about this name in verse 15? "Thus you shall say..."

a) The ________________, the God of...

b) This is My name ____________________________

c) This is My _______________________________ to all generations.

Do you see this as the personal, experiential, and salvific (saving) name of the LORD? Can you see His sovereignty in these verses?

Next, let's consider a term closely related to God's sovereignty, His Providence. At first glance, the two terms appear to be synonymous. However, in his massive work (751 pages) aptly entitled *Providence*, pastor, author, and Bible teacher, John Piper, differentiates between the two terms, stating, "The word sovereignty does not contain the idea of *purposeful action*, but the term providence does (emphasis added)."[1]

**II. Providence**

Although you may not be as familiar with this term because it is not found in Scripture, the validity of its truth, although hidden within the text, is most definitely present.[2] Much like the words *Trinity* or *discipleship*, these words may not be found in Scripture; nevertheless, they are essential biblical truths necessary for sound doctrine.

Piper's definition of providence is very helpful at this point. He explains,

> The word *providence* is built from the word *provide*, which has two parts: *pro* (Latin 'forward,' 'on behalf of') and *vide* (Latin 'to see'). So, you might think that the word *provide* would mean 'to see forward,' or 'to foresee.' But it doesn't. It means 'to supply what is needed'; 'to give substance or support.' So, in reference to God, the noun *providence* has come to mean 'the act of purposefully providing for, or sustaining and governing, the world." [3]

Equally helpful, Piper traces the definition of the word as it was used in various catechisms, and confessions throughout church history, such as:[4]

**The Heidelberg Catechism (1563)**

**Question 27. What do you understand by the providence of God?**

> **Answer.** The Almighty, everywhere-present power of God. Whereby, as it were by His hand, He still upholds heaven and earth with all creatures, and so governs them that herbs and grass, rain and drought, fruitful and barren years, meat and drink, health and sickness, riches and poverty, indeed, all things come not by chance, but by His fatherly hand.[5]

---

1 John Piper, *Providence*, (Wheaton, Ill.; Crossway, 2020), 30.

2 *Ibid.* In the footnote on this page, Piper states, "The word providence does appear once in reference to human action in Acts 24:2 in the KJV and NASB. And it occurs once in reference to God's action in Job 10:12 in the NIV and TNIV."

3 *Ibid.*, 30.

4 Note: For this section in the study, I am deeply indebted to Piper's rich and in-depth analysis of the providence of God. I highly recommend His work if you have the time and the fortitude, and you will be incredibly blessed and left in awe and worship of our God.

5 *Ibid.*, 33.

Piper then points out that the phrase "*by His fatherly hand*" makes the hidden concept, *providence*, visible.[1]

**The Belgic Confession (1561)**

**Article 13. The Doctrine of God's Providence**

> We believe that this good God, after creating all things, did not abandon them to chance or fortune but leads and governs them according to His holy will, in such a way that nothing happens in this world without God's orderly arrangement.[2]

**Westminster Larger Catechism (1648)**

**Question 18. What are the works of providence?**

> **Answer:** God's works of providence are His most holy, wise, and powerful preserving and governing all His creatures; ordering them, and all their actions, to His own glory.[3]

*In summary, and in light of all that's been said, from this point forward, we will use the simplest definition of providence, which is His *purposeful actions*.

Now, let's look in Scripture to verify everything stated so far. As you read the cross-references, record how you can see God's hidden, yet evident, providence. For this part of the study, we will trace providence in God's work in creation and redemption, but this time, we will do so from the Scriptures.

Remember, you're looking for God's purposeful *actions*.

**The Providence of God from Before the Foundation of the World**

1. John 1:1--3

Again, note the timing of the purposeful actions of God. Can you see they align with Genesis 1:1, from eternity past?

Next, let's look at His providential care in His priestly prayer just hours before the cross in these next two cross-references from John 17. Again, make note of the timing as you list facts about His providence – or purposeful actions.

2. John 17:4–5 - ______________________________________________________

3. John 17:24 - ______________________________________________________

Do you see the reason and His motive for the work He had accomplished?

4. Ephesians 1:4–6

Did you see when His purposeful activity occurred (v. 4)?

---

1 *Ibid.*

2 *Ibid.*

3 *Ibid.*, 34.

5. 2 Timothy 1:9 -

Did you notice when these acts were granted?

6. 1 Peter 1:17–20 -

7. Revelation 13:8 - ______________________________________________________

Note: The words, "the Lamb slain" is a reference to His sacrificial work on the cross.

In all these cross-references, did you happen to notice the timing of each purposeful creative, and redemptive act of God? In essence, His providence (purposeful actions) existed BEFORE He created anything and BEFORE the need for redemption.

Now, let's trace the providence of God in Creation. Remember, you're looking for God's purposeful *actions* in His creative work.

**The Providence of God in His Work of Creation**

We've already referenced Genesis 1:1, so this time, let's look at Colossians.

Colossians 1:16–17 -

Was anything left out of "all things"? Did you note His position regarding all created things?

**The Providence of God in His Work of Redemption**

Briefly explain what happened in Genesis 3:6–13?

**The First Good News Proclamation**

Genesis 3:15 -

Genesis 3:15 is the first mention of the gospel (good news) message in Scripture. Did you catch God's purposeful action and when it was promised in relation to humanity's fall? Did you also see that the gospel did not include the serpent (v. 14)? In other words, did you see the placement of His redemptive promise occurred <u>after</u> He cursed the enemy but before the curse on mankind and the earth? Did you see before the bad news (the curse), He proclaimed good news?

**Note:** If you are interested, feel free to consult the Appendix, which contains more information and questions about God's providence from Genesis, picking up with the flood to the time of Ruth. In this way, you will have access to what the people in the story of Ruth knew about God and His purposeful acts throughout Israel's history.

Now, let's look at our final biblical term and concept, the eternal counsel of God.

### III. The Eternal Counsel of God in His Work of Creation and Redemption

For this topic, instead of giving you the definition of God's eternal counsel, let's look at a few cross-references and allow the Scriptures to form the definition.

1. Look up the following cross-references and record your observations concerning the counsel of God. Instead of copying the verse, try filling in the observed fact(s). Be as concise as possible. Some of the references can be summed up in one or two words.

   a. Psalm 33:11 - ______________________________

   b. Psalm 73:24 - ______________________________

   c. Proverbs 8:14 - ______________________________

   d. Proverbs 19:21- ______________________________

   e. Isaiah 11:2 - ______________________________

   f. Isaiah 25:1 - ______________________________

   g. Isaiah 28:29 - ______________________________

   h. Isaiah 46:10b - ______________________________

   i. Jeremiah 32:19 - ______________________________

   j. Acts 2:23 - ______________________________

   k. Acts 4:28 - ______________________________

   l. Ephesians 1:11 - ______________________________

   m. Hebrews 6:17 - ______________________________

While reading these passages, did you see how the eternal counsel of God includes both His work in creation and redemption?

2. Now that you have a glimpse into the counsel of God, what are your conclusions from the Scriptures? Be sure to include what, when, where, why, and how in your final definition.

What ______________________________

When ______________________________

Where ______________________________

Why ______________________________

How ________________________________________________________________

As you review your lists, do you see humanity in the definition? In other words, what role does mankind play in the eternal counsel of God? Doesn't that bring you comfort?

Below are a few things I saw in reference to the eternal counsel of God:

What? His plans, purposes, wisdom, understanding, strength, and perfect faithfulness...

When? From eternity, which includes from before the foundation of the world, "plans formed long ago" (Isa. 25:1).

Where? Resides in the Father, Son, and Spirit and recorded in His eternal Word.

Why? For His glory and our good!

How? His omnipotent power as displayed through His Son by His Spirit and His Word.

You may have seen other things and that's great!

Now, think back to the split-screen image:

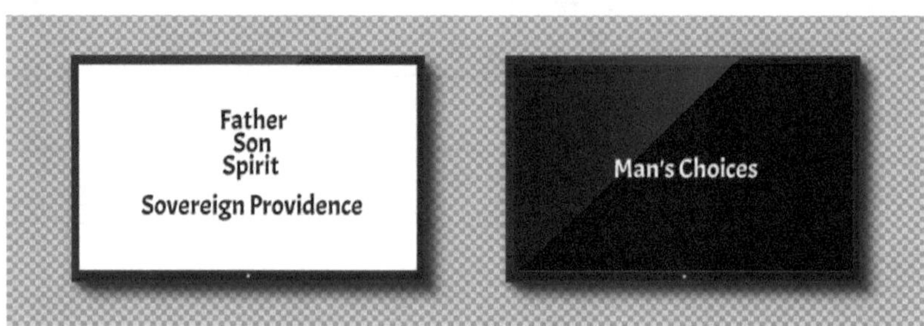


3. In summary, as you think about God's sovereignty, providence, and eternal counsel and compare it to the opening phrase in Ruth, "Now it came about...", on which side of the screen is the Divine Narrator starting the story of Ruth? ____________________________________

Are you beginning to see another realm...a previous story...much bigger than the Book of Ruth? In other words, from the eternal counsel of the Godhead, we will see our sovereign God providentially work. Watch for it.

I realize this information may cause a dilemma in your thinking. If you find yourself asking, "Since God is sovereign, and He most certainly is, then, are people truly accountable and responsible for their actions?" Great question. You find yourself in good company because countless theologians throughout history have struggled with this same predicament.

So, how do we answer this question (and every other question) except by the Word of God? Look back over your lesson as we walked through the Scriptures

a. Did you see God's sovereignty, providence, and eternal counsel?

b. Did you see man's accountability to God?

c. Did you see man's responsibility to God?

If you answered "yes," to every question, then you have your answer from Scripture, and both are true. But how can these things be true in our finite and simple minds?

Herein lies one of the greatest seemingly irreconcilable mysteries this side of heaven in Scripture. How can we reconcile a God who is completely sovereign over all His work of creation and redemption with the responsibility of man's God-ordained and God-given ability to choose?

To help, consider the words of the late pastor and theologian Charles Haddon Spurgeon. He explained the "seeming" contradiction in a sermon he preached to his church on August 1, 1858 entitled "Sovereign Grace and Man's Responsibility." He states,

> The system of truth is not one straight line, but two. No man will ever get a right view of the gospel until he knows how to look at the two lines at once. I am taught in one book to believe that what I sow I shall reap: I am taught in another place, that 'it is not of him that wills nor of him that runs, but of God that shows mercy.' I see in one place, God presiding over all in providence; and yet I see, and I cannot help seeing, that man acts as he pleases, and that God has left his actions to his own will, in a great measure. Now, if I were to declare that man was so free to act, that there was no precedence of God over his actions, I should be driven very near to Atheism; and if, on the other hand, I declare that God so overrules all things, as that man is not free enough to be responsible, I am driven at once into Antinomianism or fatalism. That God predestines, and that man is responsible, are two things that few can see. They are believed to be inconsistent and contradictory; but they are not. It is just the fault of our weak judgment. Two truths cannot be contradictory to each other.
>
> If, then, I find taught in one place that everything is fore-ordained, that is true; and if I find in another place that man is responsible for all his actions, that is true; and it is my folly that leads me to imagine that two truths can ever contradict each other. These two truths, I do not believe, can ever be welded into one upon any human anvil, but one they shall be in eternity: they are two lines that are so nearly parallel, that the mind that shall pursue them farthest, will never discover that they converge; but they do converge, and they will meet somewhere in eternity, close to the throne of God, whence all truth doth spring.[1]

Don't you love his analogy? Two truths that run parallel on earth but merge at the throne of grace! Beautiful thought, isn't it?

In the weeks ahead, you will also see these two truths side by side in the book of Ruth. I hope this information has been helpful.

After reviewing some of the main events, people, and places listed above, as I thought about their importance to the story of Ruth and began to trace back in my mind its placement within the "continuing context" of Scripture, the image of a puzzle came to mind. In fact, these two pieces (God's perspective and human perspective) provide the backdrop for the puzzle. In the weeks ahead, watch as we progressively put the puzzle pieces together in the book of Ruth and then add the story of Ruth into a much bigger, grander story in Scripture.

Think of what we have seen so far, as we put the edges of the puzzle together to form the framework for the story of Ruth.

From God's Word in Genesis 1—2, we are first introduced to our triune God: The Father, The Son, and The Holy Spirit and God's work in all creation.

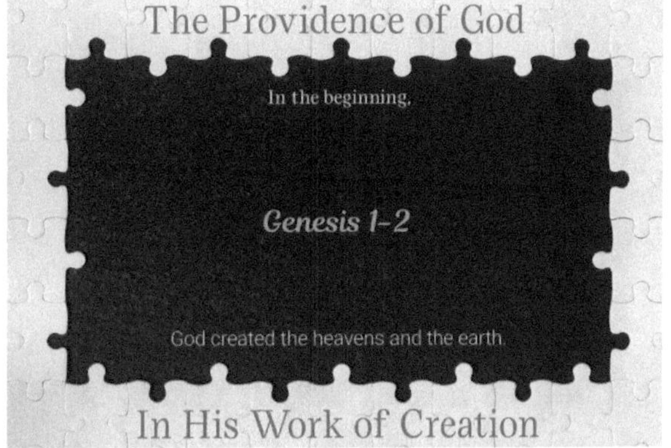


1 Charles H. Spurgeon, "Sovereign Grace and Man's Responsibility," A sermon, preached August 1, 1858 [on-line]; accessed March 19, 2023; available at https://www.spurgeon.org/resource-library/sermons/sovereign-grace-and-mans-responsibility/#flipbook/; Internet.

From Genesis 3:1–14, we discover the truth regarding mankind's temptation, the Fall, and our responses to cover, hide, and blame both God and one-another.

Did you notice the fall of humanity falls under the framework of the providence of God?

Two facts that seemingly do not coincide in our mind, right? Did you also notice the absence of the phrase "In the Work of His Creation"? That's because God is not the author of evil.

But thanks be to our God, from the first proclamation of the gospel in Genesis 3:15 until the end of the Revelation, we see our Triune God at work in our Redemption.

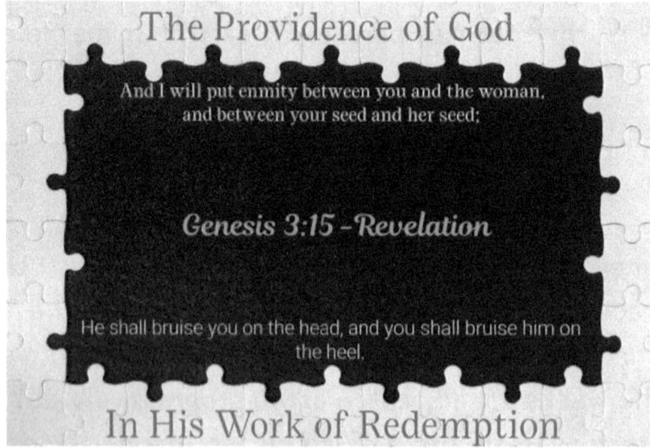


Notice, after the Fall, God's work changes from Creation (because His creative work is complete) to His work in redemption (New Creation). You see, the fall of humanity can fit into the providence of God without changing His eternal plan. In other words, the fall of humanity did not require a Plan B. God's work of redemption was set BEFORE the foundation of the world and BEFORE sin existed.

Now let's see where the book of Ruth fits within the overarching biblical framework of "the providence of God in His Work of Redemption."

Did you see how the book of Ruth sits within the framework (as every other book in the Bible) of the providence of God and His work of redemption in history?

Ultimately then, by the end of the study, in keeping with the "Complete/Canonical Context," we will look ahead and discover how the book of Ruth plays a necessary part in His story as it is framed within The Providence of God in His Work of Redemption.

## *Is there a more beautiful picture in all eternity?*

Furthermore, as you think about the progression of God's Plan, we see how the people in the Old Testament were continually looking forward to the Promised Seed (Gen. 3:15), and now, those of us in the New Testament church era keep looking back at our beautiful Savior.

In every image, we see His unfolding story as we joyfully discover that the Father has a plan to save, which will be accomplished through the work of His Son. Therefore, His unfolding plan makes Jesus Christ the central focus of God's Word and will be the foundation of this study. Be looking for Him, even if He appears to be hidden.

So now, having placed The Book of Ruth within its "continuing context," we will begin to narrow our focus in the book of Ruth while we fill in the pieces as they are given in the narrative. Let's return then to the book of Ruth and begin looking down a little more closely so we can fill in the pieces of this puzzle.

Let's begin by reading the first sentence in the Book of Ruth and fill in the second phrase: "Now it came about, in the ______________________________________"

Obviously, the Book of Ruth was placed at a particular time in Israel's history; therefore, this phrase will set the backdrop for the setting of Ruth. Let's investigate. But first, some background information.

### A Continuing Context: "The days when the judges governed"

**The Book of Judges: A Little Background Information**

Unlike the first five books of the Bible (known as the Pentateuch), the book of Judges derives its name from the central characters in the book—the judges. At first glance, the title "Judges" may cause you to think of our legal system today, where a judge presides over a particular court to decide legal matters based upon the governing law. But a closer study of the Book of Judges will indicate more of a regional, tribal, or military leader raised up by the LORD to deliver the Israelites during specific times within approximately 300-350 years in Israel's history.

Ultimately, the fact that the LORD (Yahweh) raised up each judge makes Him the true Judge of Israel during this time. Moreover, the purpose of each judgeship was salvific rather than judicial.

Additionally, no one judge ruled over all of Israel at any given time during this period. However, some of the judges the LORD raised ruled simultaneously but in different areas of the country. Given the previous information, let's jump into the Book of Judges for a brief overview.

5. Read Judges 1:1a and record the event that began the era of the Judges:

6. Now, read Judges 1:19–34. Do you see a repeated pattern as each tribe of Israel attempted to take possession of their allotted land? Record it below.

7. Did you see a shift with the tribe of Dan (v. 34)? What happened to them?

Now, you may be thinking, *Maybe the sons of Israel did not know what they were to do when they encountered the 'ites' in their region.* Exodus (34:10–14), Numbers (33:50–56), and Deuteronomy (7:1–11) each address the issue. Keep in mind, the leaders in Israel had the first five books. In other words, this was their "Bible" at the time.

8. Choose one of these places in Scripture and record your insights in the space provided. Be sure to list the Lord's instructions and what would happen if they disobeyed. The repetition in Exodus, Numbers and, Deuteronomy show how many times the LORD forewarned Israel.

**Note:** The *Asherim* represented the female counterpart to Baal. Baal was the Canaanite god of fertility, and the Ashtaroth was the Canaanite goddess of fertility, love, and war. She was the wife of Baal, according to Greek mythology.

9. Deuteronomy 7:8–10 adds something Exodus and Numbers does not. Here, you will see the LORD's motive (v. 8) and character (v. 9) behind His instructions and warning. What do you see?

Now, after reading the LORD's clear instructions as given in Exodus, Numbers, and Deuteronomy, and comparing these cross-references with Israel's pattern in Judges 1, did the children of Israel love/obey God? We can answer this question definitively in Judges 2.

10. With that in mind, read Judges 2:1–5, and record who appears in verse 1?

11. Let's pause here to help identify the "angel of the LORD." To do so, we will turn to Exodus 23. Answer the following questions using Exodus 23:20–33.

    a. Who does the LORD God promise to send to Israel (v. 20)? ____________________

b. Where will He be positioned in terms of Israel (v. 20)? ______________________

c. What will He do (v. 20)? 1) To ______________________________

and

2) To ______________________________

d. What are Israel's instruction in terms of the "angel" (v. 21)?

1) ______________________________

and

2) ______________________________

3) Do not be ____________________

For He will not ______________________________

Since, My name is ____________ (v. 21).

e. Who will "completely destroy" all the "ites" in the land (v. 23)? ______________

f. Now, read the verses 24–33. Doesn't this sound like Exodus 34:10–14; Numbers 33:50–56; and Deuteronomy 7:1–11? Do you see the link between Exodus 23:20–33 and Judges 2:1–5?

Wouldn't you agree that Israel had been forewarned many times? And they were not being sent alone because the LORD was going before them. Oh, that Israel had listened and obeyed the LORD. And wouldn't you concur we, too, have been warned, except even more so, for we have Israel's disastrous example? Oh, that we would listen and obey Him!

**Note:** This is the first of three pre-incarnate Christophanies in the book of Judges (2:1; 6:11–18; 13:3–23). A Christophany is a pre-incarnate appearance of Christ in the Old Testament.

12. Now, read Judges 2:1 again and fill in the blanks: "Now the angel of the LORD came up from ______________ to ____________________.

**Note:** One would do well to pay close attention to geography when mentioned. There are no idle words in Scripture. For example, Gilgal represents the place of meeting, listening to, and obeying God, and it was a place of celebration of God to Israel (see Joshua 4:19; 5:9–13). However, *Bochim*, which means *weeping*, represents the place of disobedience and great sadness (Judges 2:4–5).

13. As you read Judges 2:1–5, summarize what you see?

14. Now, read Judges 2:10b and record how Scripture describes Israel's next generation:

a. ______________________________

nor

b. ______________________________

Tragic, isn't it? It's terrifying to think we are one generation away from not knowing the Lord our God or His work in creation and in this case, redemption? What should that cause us to do?

15. Now, read Judges 2:11–13 and record the nature of Israel's apostasy. What do you see?

16. Read the LORD's response in verses 14–15. What did He do?

**Note:** If you were to read the rest of chapter 2, you will discover a summary of Israel's repeated cycle over the next 350 years (2:11–23).

17. Now, let's go to Judges 3:1–4. Answer the following questions using these verses.

a. Why did the LORD leave the nations (v.1)? ____________________

Notice the author of Judges lists the nations He purposefully left in verse 3.

b. What was the LORD wanting to teach Israel (v. 2)?

c. What was the purpose of the testing, according to verse 4?

**Note:** When the Lord tests His people, He does so to "squeeze" out of them what He sees in their hearts. Anything that does not look like His Son must go! There is something unique about the Lord's tests—ONLY He can pass them! And in His grace, He can and will if we let Him!

From this point forward (Judges 3:7) until the end of the book (Judges 21:25) Scripture records Israel's repeated cycle of sin/rebellion☞captivity☞crying out☞deliverance-☞rest☞sin/rebellion... for approximately 350 years.

Tragically, by the time we reach chapters 17–21, the evil and darkness of Israel are heinous. Read these chapters if you have the time and can stomach the atrocities. They represent the essence of apostasy, depravity, and utter darkness!

18. Now, before we close this section of the study, look at the following cross-references and record what you see:

a. Judges 17:6 ______________________________________________________

b. Judges 21:25 ______________________________________________________

Note: Judges 17:6 and 21:25 are the key verses necessary to unlock the meaning of the Book of Judges and perfectly describe what these days were like in Israel's history, "when there was no king in Israel."

Do you see what happens to a person or nation who "does what is right in their own eyes?" When contemplating these passages, one cannot help but think of the spiritual digression spiraling downward in Romans 1:18–32. In fact, the worst judgment of all is when God gives us over to ourselves "to do what is right in our own eyes."

Now, let's put together what we have studied so far:

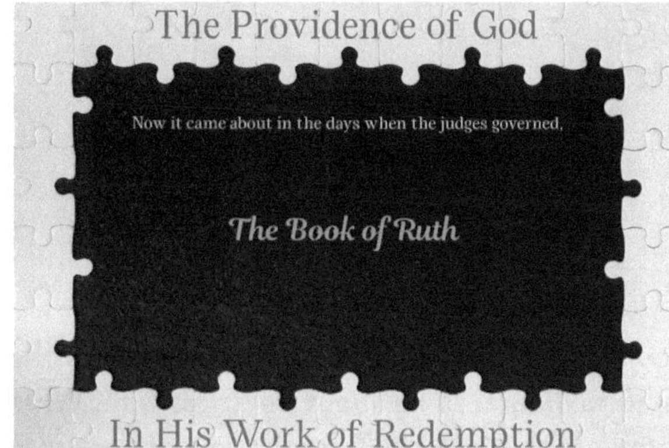


"Now it came about..." forms the framework of God's providence in the work of redemption.

And "in the days when the judges governed," becomes the dark backdrop in the puzzle of Ruth's story.

Do you see it?

19. Now, read and record the last phrase in Ruth 1:1, "______________________________."

At first glance, we might be tempted to move past this detail in the story to get to the story, but if we pause here, we can gain insight into why the Divine Narrator added this information. As we get started, let's consider a couple of questions: First, "What do you know about famines?" and second, "From where do famines come?"

Remember that the world would tell us that famines are an act of "mother nature," but is that true? Is that the biblical worldview?

Scripture records thirteen famines, which we will not cover in detail in this lesson, for our purpose is to examine how the Lord providentially used them in the lives of His people.

Let's start with the first famine recorded.

20. Read Genesis 12:10.

a. Who did the famine directly affect? ______________________________________

**Note**: The phrase stating, "Now there was a famine in the land..." should cause you to think: providence!

b. Where did Abram run for help? ______________________________

**Note**: In Scripture, historically and geographically, Egypt is a real place. However, figuratively speaking, Egypt also has a biblical connotation representing a picture of the world.

Moreover, the word *sojourn* tells us Abram's intentions because it means he was going to Egypt *temporarily*. Keep this word in mind; you will see it again in the book of Ruth.

At first glance, Abram's response seems reasonable, right? But in keeping with "continuing context," we must *look back* in Scripture to determine what the LORD had promised Abram prior to the famine.

c. Read Genesis 12:1–3. What had the LORD promised Abram in terms of taking care of him?

d. As you think about all that the LORD had promised Abram, did you find it odd that there was a famine not long afterward? Could the God who had just promised Abram blessings not make provision? Would God be true to His Word? Did you happen to notice where Abram turned when trouble came? Read Isaiah 31:1 and compare it with all you have seen in Abram's choice to "go down" to Egypt. Be sure and record your thoughts.

If you are familiar with the rest of the story in Genesis 12, you would know that Abram's decision to turn to the world rather than the LORD proved troublesome, especially when he told Sarai to lie about being his wife. What had been a temporary solution (*sojourn*) took a potentially more permanent turn when Pharaoh brought Sarai into his house (vv. 11–15).

Repeatedly in Scripture, we see the Lord revealing His character and Word to His people, and then afterward, He tests their faith regarding both. Where do you run when there's trouble?

But the LORD intervened and struck Pharaoh and his house with great plagues because of Sarai, Abram's wife" (v. 17). If you read to the end of the chapter, you will see Pharoah questioning Abram and having him escorted out of Egypt, along with Sarai and all that belonged to him (vv. 18–20).

**Note:** At first glance, it may appear that Abram profited from lying to Pharaoh. Have you ever considered that in this encounter with Pharoah, Abram acquired an Egyptian slave girl named Hagar? Talk about trouble! (See Genesis 16 for more information.) Consider also that Ishmael and his descendants (the Arabs) were a constant source of problems for Israel and are still today. Abram's disobedience proved quite costly!

Interestingly, Abraham's son Isaac would get the same test when a famine occurred in Genesis 26:1–11, but this time, the situation played out among the Philistines. Sadly, like Abraham, he failed the test, but the LORD in His lovingkindness and faithfulness intervened.

The next time we see the word *famine* is in Genesis 41, when Pharaoh has a disturbing dream, as God reveals to Pharaoh through Joseph "what He is about to do" (Genesis 41:25, 28, and 32).

If you are familiar with the story, you will remember that God used the dreams to forewarn and prepare Pharaoh and position Joseph in leadership for seven years of abundance, followed immediately by seven years of severe famine (Genesis 41).

Providentially, even Joseph's father, Jacob, and his brothers, who were still in the land of Canaan, would need the grain that had been stored in Egypt (Genesis 42—44) and eventually end up in Goshen, near Egypt (Genesis 45:10—47:27). Ultimately, God would use the famine to reveal His plan all along.

21. Look at the following references to discover God's purpose.

   a. Read Genesis 45:5, 7–8. Record God's purpose in all that happened to Joseph and the seven years of famine. What was God doing?

So, did that excuse Joseph's brothers and Potiphar's wife and all that happened to Joseph along the way? Absolutely not! Do you see the free will and responsibility of humanity within the providence of God?

Following the death of Jacob, the brothers feared Joseph would retaliate (Genesis 50: 15-18). Again, record the words of Joseph as He reveals God's ultimate purpose concerning all the things that happened.

b. Read Genesis 50:20 and record what God was doing all along.

**Note:** Clearly, God uses famine to display His judgment and His mercy. In other words, God's providential acts display His character and His Word.

Did you notice that God used the famine to test Abraham's and Isaac's faith? Would they trust God and His Word? When outwardly pressed, where would His people turn?

Furthermore, with Joseph, He used it to position or reposition His people for salvation. Do you see the connection between God's purposeful acts as He saves those who are His?

Furthermore, all throughout Israel's history, God used the potential for famine to warn Israel, for obedience to Him resulted in the salvation of His people. Disobedience would lead to their undoing.

22. Read Leviticus 26:2–5 and 14–15, and 19 and record the LORD's warning. Notice why the LORD sent famine in these verses. Record your observations.

23. Next, turn to Deuteronomy 28. Notice this chapter records the LORD'S blessings and curses. Look at verses 45–48 and record what Israel could expect and why.

Did you see in the list, hunger (v. 48)? Did you happen to catch why?

Keep these things in mind when you meet Elimelech and his family in Ruth 1:2, as well as the entire nation of Israel who had access to the warnings you just read from the examples in the Pentateuch. Remember, this was their Bible at that time.

**Note:** Later, Israel would have had access to even more truth. For example, if you are familiar with your Bible, you will recall times of severe famine recorded in the days of David (2 Sam. 21:1), Elijah (1 Kgs. 17:1, 18:2), and Elisha (2 Kgs. 4:38). Feel free if you have time to investigate these references.

Next, let's see how the LORD used famine to accomplish His purposes, specifically during the time of the prophets. Remember, these two instances are not exhaustive, but they will give us a good picture of what God is doing.

For example, in Jeremiah 14, the LORD tells Jeremiah He has sent a drought (v. 1) because of Israel's "iniquities, apostacies, and sin" (Jeremiah 14:7).

24. Read verses 11–13, and record what the LORD specifically used to punish Israel.

What three things does He use (v.12)? a. ________________________________

b. ________________________________

c. ________________________________

Similarly, Ezekiel 14 records Israel's continual idolatry and immorality (vv. 3–5), and the LORD'S call for them to repent (v. 6). However, if they refused, He forewarned what He would do.

25. Read verse 13 and record what the LORD said He would send and why.

26. Now, read verse 21. Record the four severe judgments God used against Jerusalem.

a. ________________________________

b. ________________________________

c. ________________________________

d. ________________________________ (sometimes called pestilence).

27. Now, as you process all that you have read, how did the LORD use famine in the time of the prophets?

In summary, God uses famine (and other forms of judgment) to serve two purposes in His divine providence. For those who are His, they are useful, as He uses them to "conform us into the image of His Son" (Ro. 8:29), and yet, for those who reject God's Son and His Word, His judgment awaits. Both actions are merciful. To the one who is His, it can be used to get us back on the right track when we veer off. To the one who is lost, it can cause them to cry out for salvation from judgment.

28. Now before we conclude, we must consider a different type of famine in the Scriptures. As you will discover, this famine is far more terrifying and dreadful than a lack of food. Read Amos 8:11–12. What do you see?

Can you even begin to imagine how distressing this famine would be? Could that happen to a nation or an individual today? Did you notice that the famine was for the "hearing" of the Word? In other words, it's not that they do not have the Word. But they cannot hear it. This is the state of the unbeliever and why the gift of grace through faith is so very precious.

Do you see there is a worse fate than physical death? Spiritual death is eternal! For the believer, physical death is the door to eternal life!

Finally, who would have thought the first sentence of the opening chapter of the Book of Ruth would be so pregnant with meaning? Notably, all three statements are theological.

For example:

Now it came about

in the days when the judges governed

that there was a famine in the land.

Do you see:

The Providence of God

Total Depravity of Man

God's Judgment: Punishment/Discipline to Conform?

You see, from the eternal counsel of His will, our sovereign God has been providentially at work. He continues to be actively and purposefully at work (Providence) amid humanity's instability and its dark and oppressive disobedience (total depravity) since the Fall. God may send a famine (and other catastrophes) in His mercy and judgment to cause His creation to cry out for repentance. For the unbeliever, this weeping is a cry for deliverance from the domain of darkness and sin; for the child of God, to discipline him back to Himself. Essentially, His ultimate purpose is for all humanity to "Look to Him, and be saved, for He is God and there is no other (Isa. 45:22).

And in closing, by looking in the face of the dark and harsh backdrop in the first chapter of Ruth, we must ask ourselves, "Where do you turn when times are dark?" When it appears that the heavens have been shut, do you run to the Lord, Creator of all things, or turn to His creation?

Is the Lord testing His word in your life by allowing a difficult time of famine? What does He want you to know about Himself? What does He want you to see about yourself?

In the next lesson, we will see what one family chose during this backdrop when "the days of the judges governed" when there was a "famine in the land." And as you already know, all of this is framed within the providence of God in His work of redemption. Believe it or not, things are about to get a lot darker in chapter one.

Now, before we proceed to the first chapter of Ruth, let's put all three phrases together so that we can visualize the backdrop of Ruth:

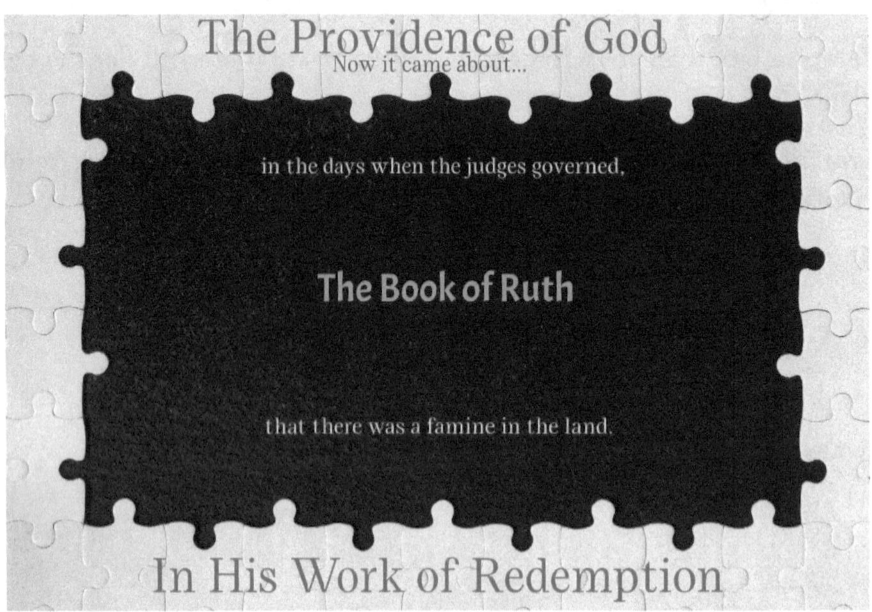


Before we continue in chapter one of Ruth, read the instructions, "How to Study the Book of Ruth," on the following two pages. These instructions will serve as a guide on how to proceed in the study.

# How to Study

## The Book of Ruth

When approaching any story in the Bible, the visual of a puzzle comes to mind. And although every individual story fits within the larger narrative of Scripture, each story is unique and comes in its own box.

So, as we begin our study in Ruth, think in these terms as we dump out the pieces and start to put them together in the order they occur in Scripture. Watch the progression as we methodically observe, interpret, and apply the story of Ruth as it unfolds in Scripture.

We will start as we would with any puzzle by putting the straight edges together first. Once the biblical framework is established, we will set the book, so to speak, in its own unique backdrop, for every story has its own distinctive beginning and background.

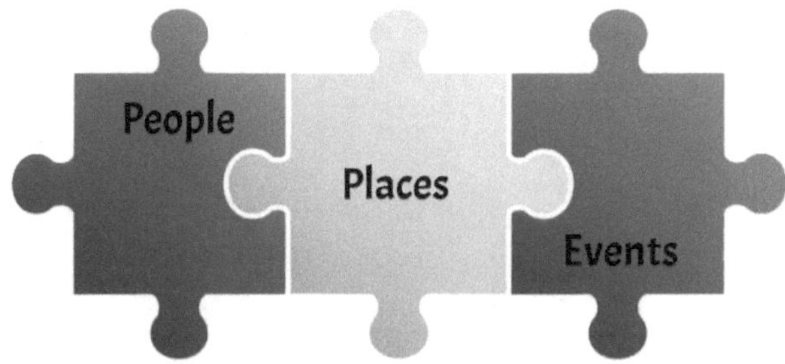


Next, we will begin to put the individual pieces together, understanding that the people, places, and events are the elements that make the story unique in a narrative.

As the pieces are added in the order they appear in Scripture, an entire scene (or section of Scripture) will become visible.

+

And as each scene is added one to another, the whole story of Ruth will begin to unfold as it happened in history. By allowing each scene to develop on its own while merging it into the developing narrative, we start to see an even bigger, grander story unfold before our eyes.

When this happens, we discover, as the psalmist declares, "The unfolding of Your Words gives light; it gives understanding to the simple" (Ps. 119:130).

Watch as we begin the story of Ruth by placing it into a much more extensive story, one we will never be fully able to comprehend this side of eternity that started before the foundation of the world, and then be amazed in the end as you will see the story culminate in a specific person, place, and event that will forever affect all of eternity's future. As I think about this, two words come to mind—Only God!

* Each lesson will cover one chapter in the book of Ruth. Due to the length of each chapter, feel free to take two weeks for each lesson or move at your own pace. And, as I used to tell my Bible students, always follow rule #1 - Never read the Bible in a hurry!

Enjoy your time in the light ☺

# Lesson 2

## The Lord's Providence: Man's Choices

RUTH 1:1B–21

Now that we have established a working framework, "The Providence of God in His Work of Redemption," and have recognized the very dark and oppressive background in which the book is set, we can start to fill in the missing pieces of the story of Ruth. Our focus this week will be Ruth 1:1b–21.

Continuing the biblical narrative, rather than focusing on an entire nation, the story concentrates on the lives of one family providentially and sovereignly placed within this very dark and oppressive time, "in the days when the judges governed" and during the time of "famine in the land" (Ruth 1:1a).

As we examine chapter one, notice the divisions within your Bible's text. You can find them by looking for the chapter's bold verse numbers in your Bible. You may or may not be aware that there were no chapter or verse divisions in the originals. Man put these divisions in place. Therefore, they are neither inspired nor infallible. Their purpose serves to be helpful for reference and quotation.

In the book of Ruth, if you look in your Bible, you will see four distinct sections in chapter one. Each section will serve as a scene within the story for this study.

As we look at each section, you will be asked to pull from the text three elements: people, places, and events. Additional information will be provided, as well as questions along the way to cause the reader to glean insights from within the text. As you observe the three elements within each scene, you will be able to accurately interpret the story of Ruth and apply the truths gathered in each section. So, let's get started.

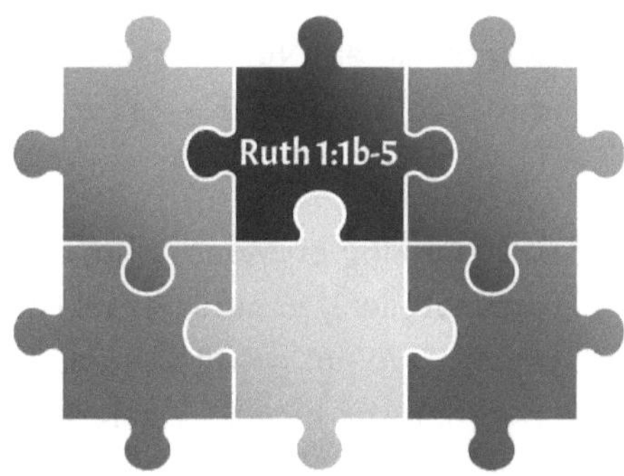


### Day One

### Scene One: Putting the Pieces Together

Begin today's lesson with prayer.

Read the first scene of the narrative, Ruth 1:1b–5 and record the people, places, and events in this section on the next page.

People

I. Who are the people in these verses? List them in the order they occur in the story. (Consider including the verse numbers.)

**Gathering Information:**

**Origin of Names**

In the Hebrew language, names had significant meanings. For example, Elimelech's name means "The King (Yahweh) is my God."[1] Naomi means "kindness, pleasantness, sweetness."[2] The names of their sons are uncertain; however, Ruth 4:10 helps identify who married whom in verse 4.

1. What do you see? Mahlon's wife - ________________________

Chilion's wife - ________________________

**The Ephrathites**

In verse 2, there is mention of the "Ephrathites of Bethlehem in Judah." You will also find them mentioned in Genesis 35:19. In this phrase, the narrator has just provided the people group called the Ephrathites, the town of Bethlehem, and the territory or tribe of Judah—all in that one little phrase.

**The Moabites**

We will start with their origin. To discover their lineage, you will need to go to the book of beginnings, Genesis.

1. Read Genesis 19 for context and record your observations from verses 30–38.

2. To understand the Moabites' relationship with Israel, Numbers 22–26; 31:8, 16 is helpful. Due to a large amount of material, please allow me to summarize the main events for brevity. Feel free to read these passages yourself if you have the time.

The account in Numbers 22 begins with Balak, the king of Moab, who, out of fear, sent some of his servants to hire Balaam (the Midianite), a soothsayer (fortuneteller), to curse Israel (Num. 22:3–6). Numbers 22:9 records that God came to Balaam and warned him, saying. "Do not go with them; you shall not curse the people; for they are blessed." So, Balaam refused to go with the men the king of Moab sent (Num. 22:13–14).

Then the king of Moab sent additional men of distinction and offered more money to hire Balaam to curse Israel (Num. 22:15–18). With God's permission, Balaam goes with the men this time; however, he was instructed only to say what God told him (Num. 22:20).

---

1 Edward F. Campbell, J., *Ruth: A New Translation with Introduction, Notes, and Commentary*; Vol. 7, (New Haven, Conn.: Yale University Press, 2008), 52.

2 Daniel I. Block, *The New American Commentary: Judges/Ruth* Vol. 6, (Nashville, TN.: Broadman & Holman Publishers, 1999), 625.

From Numbers 22:41—24:9, Balak, the king of Moab, took Balaam, the soothsayer, to three different high places (Baal worship), and each time, Balaam blessed Israel rather than cursing them as he had been paid to do. At first, it looks like Balaam is genuinely obedient to the LORD until you read Numbers 25:1–3 and see the influence his counsel had on the children of Israel.

a. Read Numbers 25:1–3 and record your observations.

Then, the anger of the LORD burned against Israel that day, killing 24,000 men (Num. 25:4–9).

b. Next, read Numbers 31:8 and record what happened to Balaam, the soothsayer.

c. Read Numbers 31:15–16. What had Balaam done to deserve death?

You see, Balaam's "obedience" not to curse the Israelites "appeared" righteous. But Balaam loved money, and he could be bought for a price. Rather than curse Israel, as the king of Moab requested, Balaam showed the king of Moab how to trap the Israelites by using the Moabite women. He knew that the women would turn the hearts of the Israelite men to their gods. His counsel, in turn, would evoke God's wrath upon Israel with God passing judgment upon Israel, and Balaam knew that. Pretty diabolical and devious, wouldn't you say?

3. Now, record what the LORD said to Israel concerning Moab:

a. Deuteronomy 2:9 -

b. Deuteronomy 23:3–6 –

4. Now, let's look at the Moabites in a more current light for Ruth's study, "in the days when the judges governed," in the Book of Judges.

   a. Judges 3:12, 14 (context vv. 12–30) -

   b. Judges 11:17 – Notice what happened when Israel asked permission to pass through their land on the way to Canaan.

5. In summary, what is the relationship between Moab and Israel, having gathered all this information?

Next, we will explore the significant places in Scene One.

II. What places are mentioned in this section?

Gathering Information:

The word *Bethlehem* comes from two Hebrew words: *beyt* (house) and *lehem* (bread).[1]

1. If you put the two words together, you have _______________ of ________________.

**Note:** In this section, we will include facts about timing when it is necessary. Essential to timing, is the key word, *sojourn*. The Hebrew word for sojourn (*gur*) is a verb meaning "to dwell as a foreigner; to seek hospitality with." The word carries the idea of a more temporary nature instead of settling down or permanence. (For example, Israel would have sojourned in the wilderness. Believers can also be called sojourners on earth awaiting our eternal home with the Lord.)

2. Now, record from verse 4, how long they "sojourned" in Moab? _____________________

Please pause to consider the length of this amount of time. Keep that in mind as we progress.

3. Now, let's visually trace their journey using the map below.

The territory of Moab was to the east of Bethlehem. It was largely mountainous terrain with some plateau land toward the Arnon River.[2] If you look closely, you can see the line tracking the way they would have had to travel.

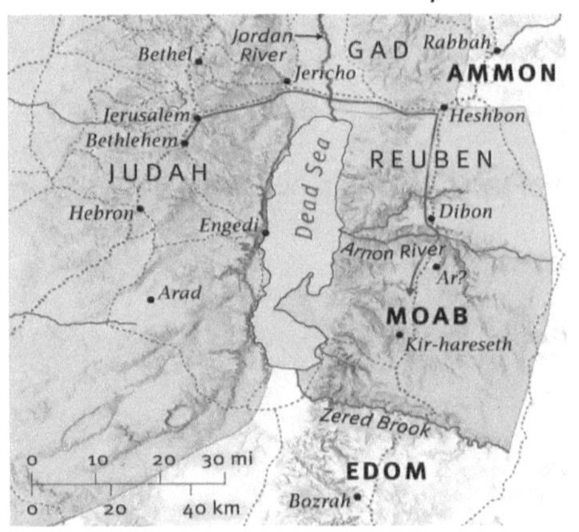


Moab was approximately 60-75 miles from Bethlehem. The journey would have taken approximately 7-10 days on foot.

**Note:** The Hebrew verb *sa'ar*, translated "bereft" in verse 5 needs our attention, and it means "to remain, to be left, to spare."[3] The verb and the nouns that derive from it (se'ar and se'eriyt) play a key role in developing the remnant theme that unfolds and evolves throughout Old Testament history. From the early beginnings of salvation history in Genesis through to the end of the Old Testament and beyond, God has sovereignly acted to preserve for Himself a remnant of people who will worship Him alone (Gen. 7:23; 32:8 [9]; 1 Kgs. 19:18; Ezra 9:8; Isa. 4:3; 11:11, 16; 37:31; Ezek.

1 Warren Baker, ed., *The Complete Word Study Dictionary Old Testament*, 133.

2 *Ibid.*, 578.

3 Warren Baker, ed., *The Complete Word Study Dictionary Old Testament*, 1087.

9:8; Zeph. 3:12; and Rom. 11:5: emphasis added)."[1] Keep this in mind as you interpret how the narrator describes Naomi.

Events

III. Now, beginning with verse 1b–5, list the events in this scene as they occurred. Consider including the verse numbers for later reference.

Now, after observing the text and with the additional information, let's make some connections as we begin to interpret Ruth 1:1b–5 by asking a series of questions, followed by comments as needed.

**Putting the Pieces Together**

**Note:** Typically, the narrator rarely passes or definitively states a moral judgment in a Hebrew story. However, enough internal clues (expressed or left out) are provided and should be helpful when interpreting the truth.

1. What are your thoughts concerning Elimelech taking his family from Bethlehem to *sojourn* in Moab during the famine in Israel (Ruth 1b–2)? Keep in mind the length of their stay. Be thorough in your answer and use all the information previously provided to help.

2. Have you considered what it would mean for Elimelech to choose to leave Bethlehem? What all might that imply? What would it mean for himself, his wife, and his two sons? Think of the irony in the meaning of his name and the times in which he lived, when there was no king in Israel, and "each man did what was right in his own eyes" (Judg. 21:25).

3. After establishing the origin of famines in Scripture in our previous lesson and how God uses them, specifically in the lives of His people, is it odd to you that the story begins with a "famine" in the "house of bread?" Considering Elimelech's response to his circumstances, do you think this is just a physical famine, or does the famine have spiritual implications as well? Any thoughts?

1 *Ibid.*, 1088.

4. Even though we are not told from the text how long Elimelech was in Moab before he died, what are your thoughts about the storyteller's timing in mentioning his death (v.3) following the information about remaining in Moab? Could God's providence be at work? Deuteronomy 32:39 might be helpful as you process your thoughts.

5. The narrator's choice of the words "sojourned" (v. 1) and "remained" (v.2) are telling. What do you think he is trying to communicate? As you process this question, consider that the choice to "sojourn" was away from God and His people. Thoughts?

   a. Now, view these two terms in light of sin. Think about the times in our life when we choose to compromise for a little while, and then how we can find ourselves remaining or trapped in that sin. In other words, sometimes, we can choose to "sojourn" temporarily away from God and His people and then find ourselves years later, full of regret and either unable or unwilling to return. Do not miss the subtlety of sin and its deceptive power. Any thoughts about turning away, even briefly at first, from God to something or someone else?

Have you ever considered the subtlety of sin? Have you ever heard the saying, "Sin will take you farther than you want to go, keep you longer than you want to stay, and cost you more than you want to pay." Do you think that applies here? Keep in mind, one of the simplest definitions for sin is to "not choose God." Was anyone in scene one choosing the Lord?

6. Look at the wording in verse 4 concerning Naomi's sons. Any thoughts about their choices?

**Note:** Anytime you encounter the wording in Scripture where someone is "choosing for themselves" or "making for themselves," you can bet there will be trouble.

7. As you process the marriages of the two sons and the length of time they lived in Moab, do you find it interesting that their unions produced no children? Do you think Providence was at work here? As you think about this question, consider passages like: Psalm 127:3, Genesis 16:2; 25:21; and 1 Samuel 1:6 to help and record your thoughts.

**Note:** I realize that these questions and portions of Scripture may be excruciating to consider if you are struggling with infertility or, maybe, still single. In no way do I want to be insensitive here. The pain is real and can be all-consuming. However, if we examine all of Scripture, these truths must be factored in. When the truth from Scripture hurts deeply, we must factor in the framework of God's providence in His work of redemption. And although it does not feel like He is saving us when He allows difficult situations, we are called to trust Him as God and ask the Lord to cause us to bow, even when it is the last thing, we may feel like doing.

I don't know if you're familiar with William Cowper, an English poet and hymn writer in the 18th century, or the poem he wrote as he struggled on and off in his life with deep periods of depression. But the Lord used his affliction to write many beautiful poems and hymns. The two most famous hymns he wrote include "God Moves in a Mysterious Way" and "There is a Fountain Filled with Blood."

At this point, I think it would be helpful to pause and read the hymn "God Moves in a Mysterious Way."

God moves in a mysterious way
His wonders to perform:
He plants His footsteps in the sea,
And rides upon the storm.

Deep in unfathomable mines
Of never-failing skill,
He treasures up His bright designs,
And works His sovereign will.

Ye fearful saints, fresh courage take;
The clouds ye so much dread
Are big with mercy, and shall break
In blessings on your head.

**Judge not the Lord by feeble sense,**
**But trust Him for His grace;**
**Behind a frowning providence**
**He hides a smiling face** (emphasis mine).

His purposes will ripen fast,
Unfolding every hour:
The bud may have a bitter taste,
But sweet will be the flower.

**Blind unbelief is sure to err,**
**And scan His work in vain;**
**God is His own Interpreter,**
**And He will make it plain** (emphasis mine).[1]

My prayer, if you are personally struggling because these words have hit hard or maybe just a bit too close to

1 William Cowper, "God Moves in a Mysterious Way," Hymnal.net accessed March 23, 2023, available at https://www.hymnal.net/en/hymn/h/675. Public domain.

home, is that you will allow the words in this hymn and the book of Ruth to minister to you and begin to heal your heart.

Although it is extremely sad that William Cowper suffered so intensely, I will be eternally grateful that in and through his pain, he shared these hymns with us.

Moreover, when I think of Cowper and scores of other saints throughout history and even today, who choose to minister from their pain and struggles, I am reminded of what Paul said in 2 Corinthians 1:3–4.

8. Pause here to consider these verses and record your observations from the text.

From these verses and stories like Cowper, are you beginning to see that Providence always has a saving purpose as He sovereignly acts?

Suffice it to say for now, as we progress in the story; you will discover how their lack of children, which was necessary to carry on the name of Elimelech and his family, works in an amazingly salvific (saving) way. Just wait; there is so much more to the story ahead.

9. As you combine Ruth 1:3 and 5, what has entered and seems to dominate the narrative?

Can any of you identify with Naomi?

Has death ever intruded into your life? Is it dominating your thoughts, actions, and emotions (also known as your heart)? We must pause here to think about Naomi and her situation.

Can any of you even imagine the magnitude of her loss? Her entire family has been taken. And what is even harder to fathom, it has been at the hand of the Lord, with whom she once had sweet fellowship.

What is she to do? How is she to process all of this? How would you? What do you do when the death of a loved one seems untimely and, worse, out of order? Shouldn't the child bury the parent? These things are devastatingly overwhelming to consider, but this is precisely where we find Naomi. Ponder these things and place yourself in the shoes of Naomi. For some of you, you don't have to ponder long; Providence has placed you there now.

If this is where you or someone you know and love finds yourself, keep prayerfully looking to the Lord and His Word. The Book of Ruth may just be what Providence will use to heal your heart.

10. Now, consider the use of the word "bereft" (1995 NASB) in terms of the narrator's description of Naomi. By using this specific word, what is the narrator communicating?

11. Now, did you notice the narrator chose to focus on Naomi in verse 5? Why is there no mention of Ruth or Orpah at this point? Wasn't their loss significant too? Do you have any thoughts as to why Naomi is the center at this point in the story?

Note: The death of Naomi's husband and two sons was not only overwhelmingly tragic, but it also carried social, economic, and spiritual ramifications. Remember, there were no government institutions, Medicaid plans, or external help at this point in history, and their death meant alienation, destitution, and no spiritual head or leadership. She was in real trouble, and she knew it.

12. Before we leave Scene One, are there any additional thoughts or lingering questions that come to mind? Jot them below.

**Some concluding thoughts and questions:**

Did you find it striking that the storyline begins with an Israelite man, Elimelech, whose name means, "The King (Yahweh) is my God," taking his entire family from the "house of bread" and away from God's people, to seek refuge from the famine with the enemies of Israel?

Do you think his name and actions matched when the circumstances in his life began to squeeze him? Did you see where he ran for help? Do you think he might have been taking matters into his own hands?

When the Lord orchestrates your circumstances where you find yourself at your wit's end, are you aware that the He is on the other end?

Do you seek God's perspective in times of darkness, instability, fear, and uncertainty?

Is He the first place you seek refuge, or do you tend to run to man or the world for help?

Did you notice that no one in the first scene seeks help from the Lord? No one is praying for the Lord to intervene and seeking the His perspective from His Word. Keep in mind throughout the narrative, they had the Pentateuch.

Reflecting on Ruth 1:1b–5, we see that Elimelech's failure to recognize the famine as the God's discipline on a nation that had broken His covenant led to dire consequences. When God disciplines His people, we are faced with choosing to turn towards Him or away. Instead of walking by faith in God's promises, Elimelech decided to walk by sight. Moab offered more from his perspective, at least temporarily. However, his decision led to a sojourn solution that affected his family for the next ten years and ended in death.

We, too, can be like Elimelech. Times of difficulty can cause our hearts to wander to the "Moab" in our lives, which always looks promising at first but can lead to death. Even if we make a "temporary" decision and choose to walk by sight, beware of the "Moab" solutions in your life. Be careful of sin's subtle lures. At first, it may seem reasonable, harmless, and temporary. Let Elimelech's choice be a tender warning to continue to walk by faith and not by sight. Heed the disciplines of the Lord and "Look to Him" for salvation (Isaiah 45:22) from the difficulties in this life.

**What About You?**

Where do you turn when life is difficult? Is there a "Moab" in your life at present? Run back to the Savior! I can promise, He is waiting.

## Days Two and Three

## Scene Two: Putting the Pieces Together in Ruth 1:6–14

In the next two days of study, we will focus our attention on Ruth 1:6–14.

1. Begin today's lesson with prayer.

2. Read the second scene of the narrative, Ruth 1:6–14, and record the people, places, and events in this section below.

I. Who are the people in these verses? List them in the order they occur in the story. (Consider including the verse numbers.)

Next, record the significant place in scene two.

II. What place is mentioned in this section? Be careful; it may be difficult to see at first. Look closely at the wording used.

III. Now, beginning with verse 6, list the events in this scene as they occurred. Consider including the verse numbers.

**Gathering Information:**

1. Start by thinking about the arduous journey the women made alone through mountainous terrain. Put yourself in their shoes as they make that long trek to Bethlehem.

**Thoughts:**

2. As you listed the events in verses 6–14, did you see a repeated word? ___________________

In Scene Two (1:6–14), Scene Three (1:15–18), Scene Four (1:19–21), and Scene Five (1:22) there is a key word necessary to unlock the meaning of the entire remainder of chapter one. You will find that the Hebrew verb šûb, or a derivative of the word is used twelve times in verses 6, 7, 8, 10, 11, 12, 15 (2 times), 16, 21, 22 (2 times).

**Note:** This Hebrew word (*šûb*), translated "return" repeatedly in Ruth chapter 1, is also the word for *repentance*,[1] which opens the interpretation to more than just a physical geographical return from one place to another.

3. Due to the number of times, šûb is used in this section (vv. 6, 7, 8, 10, 11, and 12), let's look at each instance to understand its importance and with what it is associated. Record your insights below.

**Note:** In reference to Naomi's first speech (1:8), we are introduced to a key theological term in the book, *hesed* (kindly). Sometimes the Hebrew word *hesed* is translated, "lovingkindness." Old Testament Hebrew scholar, Daniel Block, explains the word beautifully, stating,

> Hesed is one of Yahweh's most treasured characteristics. It is one of those Hebrew words whose meaning cannot be captured in one English word. This is a strong relational term that wraps up in itself an entire cluster of concepts, all the positive attributes of God—love, mercy, grace, kindness, goodness, benevolence, loyalty, covenant faithfulness; in short, that quality that moves a person to act for the benefit of another without respect to the advantage it might bring to the one who expresses it.[2]

4. Look at Psalm 136 where the word *hesed* is used twenty-six times and translated "lovingkindness." Notice with what it is associated in each verse. Jot down a few (or all) of the things listed in the psalm. As you make the list, see if you can put them within categories.

1 Warren Baker and Gene Carpenter, eds., *The Complete Word Study Dictionary Old Testament*, 1108.

2 Block, *The New American Commentary: Judges/Ruth* Vol. 6, 605.

Did you notice that all the things listed fit into two distinct categories: His work in creation and redemption?

Did you also see that the motive behind each is His lovingkindness (*hesed*)? Who is like the LORD our God? Did you also see how His lovingkindness is directly linked with His eternality? And that verses 1–3 and 26 serve as bookends, which should serve to evoke our response of thanksgiving?

Is the motive behind your work filled with love and gratitude to God? That can be true only if God is the source of your work.

Now, let's return to Ruth 1:8–13a to gather more vital information to help you with interpretation.

5. First, if you haven't already, carefully record Naomi's two speeches in verses 8–13a.

I. Naomi's First Speech

Naomi's request: ________________________________________________ (v. 8)

Naomi's appeal: "May the ____________ ____________ ____________ with you as you have dealt with the dead and with me" (v. 8).

"May the ____________ ____________ that you may ____________

____________, each in the house of her husband" (v. 9).

Naomi's action: ______________________________ (v.9).

Naomi, Ruth, and Orpah's response: __________________________________ (v. 9)

Ruth and Orpah's Response: ________________________________________

________________________________________ (v. 10).

II. Naomi's Second Speech

Naomi's request: ________________________________________________(v. 11).

Naomi's rhetorical questions:

#1 - ________________________________________________? (v. 11)

#2 ________________________________________________? (v. 11)

Naomi's request: ________________________________________________ (v. 12).

Naomi's rhetorical questions:

#3 - ________________________________________________

________________________________________________? (vv. 12b–13a).

#4 - ________________________________________________? (v. 13a).

Naomi's personal evaluation regarding her situation: ________________________

_______________________________ (v. 13b).

What reason does Naomi give for her evaluation? ____________________________

_______________________________________________________(v. 13b).

**Note:** In Naomi's speech to her daughters-in-law, she has one request, *return* (vv. 8, 11, and 12). Clearly, she is urging them both to remarry (v. 13a). However, included in her rhetorical questions, she mentions the absurdity of having another son, and even if that were possible, it would be too long for them to wait (v. 12b–13a). You may be asking, "Why is she talking this way? To what is she referring?" Deuteronomy 25:5–10 will help you understand her reasoning.

6. Look at Deuteronomy 25:5–10 and observe the text. Be detailed in your examination and list the facts below.

**Note:** In Scripture, Deuteronomy 25:5–10 is referred to as the levirate marriage guidelines. The word *levirate* comes from the Latin term *levir,* meaning husband's brother. Keep this in mind, for the information will prove helpful later in the story.

Now that we have gathered some pertinent information let's proceed to interpretation.

**Putting the Pieces Together**

1. With what r whom would you associate Naomi's ability to "hear" in the land of Moab that the LORD had visited His people in giving them food (v.6)?

2. What is the LORD doing when He opens the Word to your heart by His Spirit? What is He granting?

3. What does "hearing" about the LORD and His work in Bethlehem evoke within Naomi? Think about what comes as a result of "hearing the Word" (Romans 10:17).

Do you see how the Spirit of the LORD caused Naomi to hear the word, and in doing so, He granted repentance and gave her the faith to believe?

4. Now, in reference to Naomi's speeches and the dialogue between her and her daughters-in-law, answer the following questions:

   a. Did you notice the phrases "May the LORD deal kindly with you" (v. 8) and "May the LORD grant that you may find rest" (v. 9)? As you consider each question and factor in the term, *hesed* and how Ruth used it in (v.8), what is Naomi doing and how would you interpret this portion of her first speech?

   b. Did you notice anything unique about Ruth and Orpah's response in verse 10?

   c. How would you interpret Naomi's second speech and the rhetorical questions she asked?

   d. What are your thoughts regarding Naomi's personal evaluation in verse 13b? Is she blaming the LORD or is she stating a fact from her perspective?

5. Now, let's address Naomi's insistence that her daughters-in-law return to Moab. If you are like me, you might have thought at first glance, "Why would she counsel them to go back if she loved them?"

To think through this portion (1:8–9, 11–13a), consider and compare it in light of Jesus's words in Mark 8:34 and Mark 10:29–30. What are your observations?

The call to follow Christ is indeed costly, but if you have ever truly wholeheartedly followed Him, you may find that the highest cost is not what it costs you directly but what it will cost those you love most. When your obedience directly affects others, particularly your spouse and children, you will soon discover a completely different level of costliness.

6. In Naomi's speeches, there is a reference to the LORD and, specifically, the levirate marriage principles (Deut. 25:5–6), which signifies a turning point for her. What do you see in Naomi in Scene Two that was missing in the first scene (Ruth 1b–5)?

7. And finally, Scene Two closes with a very moving response from Naomi, Ruth, and Orpah in verse 14. What do you see? Note the response of each.

We will pick up here tomorrow.

## Day Four

### Scene Three: Putting the Pieces Together in Ruth 1:15–18

Today we will be focused on the third scene in chapter one. We will look intently at the three women mentioned and each of their decisions.

1. Begin today's lesson with prayer.

2. Read the third scene of the narrative, Ruth 1:15–18 and record the people, places, and events in this section below.

I. Who are the people in these verses? List them in the order they occur in the story. (Consider including the verse numbers.)

Next, record the significant place in scene three.

II. What place is mentioned in this section? (Hint: It's the same as in scene two.)

III. Now, beginning with verse 15, list the events in this scene as they occurred. Consider including the verse numbers.

**Gathering Information:**
In this scene, the only additional information necessary is the definition of salvation.

Note: Salvation, when defined biblically, must include three tenses: past, present, and future.

| Tense | Theological Term | What's Happening to You? |
|---|---|---|
| Past | Justification | "I *have been* saved from the PENALTY of sin." |
| Present | Sanctification | "I *am being* saved from the POWER of sin." |
| Future | Glorification | "I *will be* saved from the PRESENCE of sin." |

**Justification** is an act of God whereby He declares, *in a moment of time*, that we are righteous.

**Sanctification** is an act of God whereby He is in the *process* of conforming us into the image of His Son by the power of the Spirit as we surrender and obey the Word.

**Glorification** is an act in the *future* whereby God saves us eternally and entirely from our enemies: the world, our flesh, and Satan.

Salvation, whether past, present, or future, is *wholly* a work of God (Ps. 3:8; 62:1; Jon. 2:9; Rev. 19:1).

With these things in mind, let's begin to interpret Ruth 1:15–18.

**Putting the Pieces Together**
1. First, while listing the events above, could you see the different choices made?

If so, list the choices in verses 15–16. What do you see?

Orpah - ______________________________________

and

______________________________________ (v. 15).

Ruth – Where you go, __________________________________

Where you lodge, ______________________________

______________________________

and

______________________________

2. Now, compare these two things with what they both said earlier to Naomi in verse 10. What has been added to the choice?

3. Now, look at Ruth 1:7 and let's consider the place where these decisions were made. What do you see?

Do you see that somewhere between Moab and Bethlehem, Ruth and Orpah were at the crossroads of what seemed a temporal decision physically and yet, spiritually, it was an eternal choice? Consider Naomi's prayer in verses 8–9, when her appeal was to the LORD on their behalf. Who was working His plan of redemption, and to whom did He give ears to hear based upon Ephesians 2:1?

When I read Ruth 1:15–18, a picture immediately comes to mind. What do you see as you consider the following visual and compare it with these verses? Record your observations below.

4. As you think about Ruth's choice, do you see confession and repentance in her words (vv. 16–17)? Explain your answer.

5. Now, look at 1 Thessalonians 1:9 and compare Paul's description of the believers in Thessalonica with what Ruth, the Moabitess, said. What do you see?

6. Now, in light of Ruth 1:6–18, do you see that there were actually three choices made in scene 3? Record your observations.

7. In terms of salvation, as you contemplate what happened to both Naomi and Ruth, how would you describe each? What do you see?

Praise God, Naomi and Ruth were saved, but what about Orpah? Does Scripture shed light on her situation? Have you ever encountered an Orpah? She represents the person who walks alongside the Lord for a while, only to depart later. Where do such people go?

Let's turn to Scripture for answers.

8. To help us understand, see Mark 4, where Jesus gives the parable of the four soils. Read the parable in Mark 4:3–9 and then read His interpretation in verses 14–20. Answer the following questions:

   a. Which soil represents Orpah's heart and why?

   b. Which of the four soils represent the hearts of Ruth and Naomi? In your answer, please include why, using Mark 4 as a proof text.

## Day Five

### Scene Four: Putting the Pieces Together in 1:19–21

1. Begin today's lesson with prayer.
2. Read the fourth scene of the narrative, Ruth 1:19–21 and record the people, places, and events in this section below.

I. Who are the people in these verses? List them in the order they occur in the story. (Consider including the verse numbers.)

Next, record the significant place in scene four.

II. What place is mentioned in this section?

III. Now, beginning with verse 19, briefly list the events in this scene as they occurred. Consider including the verse numbers.

**Gathering Information:**
Before we get too far in the study, let's pause to gather further insight into understanding the Hebrew narrative. At this point, I gladly defer to Sinclair Ferguson for his expertise. Consider the following information as we contemplate where we are in the narrative. He explains:

> One of the characteristics of Old Testament narrative—indeed, of any good story—is that it has a center point, which is often the turning point. That is why, in Hebrew narratives, the most important thing often lies as the center of a passage or even of a single verse.
>
> We see this in many of the psalms. At the beginning of the psalm the writer is going down—into difficulties, doubts, even despair. But then the psalm ends with his spirits lifted up and his heart encouraged. The key to interpreting the change is to notice what lies at the center of the psalm, where the turning point comes, and to observe what causes it.
>
> The same is true of this story. It begins and ends in Bethlehem (vv. 1, 22). But its center point lies in what takes

place between Moab and Bethlehem. This is a turning point, geographically and also spiritually. We might even say it is the conversion point.[1]

The pattern to which Dr. Ferguson is referring is called chiasm in literature. A chiasm is a literary structure where words or concepts are repeated in reverse order forming a pattern (like English poetry) that follows, for example, A, B, C, D—D, C, B, A. These are commonplace in Hebrew literature, especially the narratives and Psalms, to help the reader identify the central words or truth. What the reader must identify in any given story is the main turning point of the story.

1. So, considering where we are so far in the study, what are your thoughts concerning the "center" or turning point in the book of Ruth? What reference would you insert and why?

Do you see that Ruth's profession in Ruth 1:16–17 is the turning point in the narrative?

And rightly so because every believer's story has a turning point—from death to life! And now, everything that happens until the end of the story corroborates with what Paul confidently told the believers in Philippi when he stated, "He who began a good work in you will perfect until the day of Christ Jesus" (Phil. 1:6).

2. So, if you were to think on a much larger scale, in these terms of the Bible as one extensive Hebrew narrative, what would be the central figure and turning point event between the Old and New Testaments?

Next, to better interpret the fourth scene, some additional information may be helpful in your understanding of the verbs.

**Note:** The phrases "dealt very bitterly'" "brought me back," and "has afflicted" are all verbs in the *hifʿîl* stem, which indicates "the causative sense of verbs." In other words, Naomi clearly states that the LORD is the cause of all that has happened to her.

Now with this information, let's begin to interpret all that we see in Scene Four (Ruth 1:19–21).

**Putting the Pieces Together**

1. First, when you see the words, "and it came about" in verse 19, what comes to mind?

Have you noticed that the only *overt* mention of the LORD in the story is from the mouth of Naomi? First in her prayer in verses 8–9 and then again in her analysis of His treatment toward her in verses 13, 20, and 21.

2. Having examined what she said about the LORD in her prayer in the previous lesson, let's pick up with what Naomi says about the LORD in terms of His dealings with her from her perspective. Record what Naomi says about the LORD <u>and</u> to whom she says these things.

---

1 Sinclair Ferguson, *Faithful God: An Exposition of the Book of Ruth* (Bryntirion, Bridgend, Wales, UK: Bryntirion Press, 2005), pp.22–23.

a. Ruth 1:13b -

b. Ruth 1:20 -

c. Ruth 1:21 -

Now let's look a little more closely at each statement separately.

3. Considering what Naomi says to her daughters-in-law, do you think she is blaming the LORD or simply stating the truth from God's Word? In other words, is she assessing the LORD's actions from her perspective or His? To help answer these questions and summarize your answer, read Deuteronomy 28:1–2, 5, 8, 12–14, contrasted with verses 15, 17, 24, 33, 38–40, 45–47. And again, Deuteronomy 32:39 and 47. Briefly validate your answer with Scripture.

Do you see that Naomi's words coincide with what the LORD had previously stated? Therefore, can you see she is evaluating her situation with what God said about Himself (Deut. 32:39) and His Word? Do you think the One who caused her to "hear" about the food in Bethlehem has also opened her ears to His Word?

4. Now, let's examine her encounter with the women in Bethlehem.

   a. First, who initiated the conversation, and what was stated?

   b. Why do you think the women asked Naomi that specific question? Think through the length of time she had been away, the toll death had taken, and the meaning of her name as you answer. Record your observations below.

5. Now, rather than recording Naomi's response as you did earlier, let's pause to examine *how* she answered. First, did you notice in verses 20–21, Naomi mentions two names of God? Record the two names she acknowledged. a. ________________________

b. ________________________

**Note:** An in-depth study of the Names of God would reveal that each specific name corresponds to man's need. This fact will be helpful anytime you see a particular name mentioned.

6. In our first lesson, you may recall that we touched on God's covenant name, LORD (*Yahweh*). But you may not be familiar with the Hebrew name, *El Shaddai*, translated as God Almighty. To gather information about this name, let's go to the first place in Scripture, where God Himself introduces it.

a. Read Genesis 17 and answer the following questions:

1) First, what do you learn about Abram in verse 1?

**Note:** Sarah is ten years younger than Abram, making her 89 when God reveals His name as God Almighty. This information will prove necessary in our attempt to grasp the meaning of this particular name of God.

2) What does God Almighty instruct Abram concerning this name in verse 1?

a) ________________________________________

and

b) ________________________________________

3) What is God Almighty establishing between Abram in verse 2b?

4) Record Abram's response in verse 3. What did he do?

5) Now, read verses 4–9. Do you notice the phrases "As for Me" and "Now as for you"? List the facts concerning each below:

| **As for Me...** | **As for you...** |
|---|---|
| I will ________________________________ | ________________________________ |
| I will ________________________________ | You and your ______________________ throughout their generations (v.9). |
| I will ________________________________ | |
| I will ________________________________ | |
| I will ________________________________ | |

I will ________________________________

Did you happen to notice that God Almighty has the bigger list? Do you see that God Almighty is connected to the covenant He had made with Abraham, and later Isaac, and Jacob? Would this also apply in Naomi's day?

When you think about God's covenant with Abram, what's even more amazing, is that Abram would not be able to do his part without God. So basically, only God Almighty has the power to accomplish both parts!

6) Now, record what God Almighty does with Abram's name and why in verse 5.

7) Now, look at verses 15–16. What does God Almighty do in this verse and why?

**Note:** Name changes in Scripture are always noteworthy. It signifies that a more significant change in identity has occurred. It is incredibly weighty when the One who changes your name is God Almighty, the only One with the power to do so. For example, by changing Abram and Sarai's names, the Almighty is adding Himself and a portion of His covenant name, Yahweh (**יהוה**), to their name.

One of the sweetest explanations of this account comes from author and Bible teacher Kay Arthur, who explains,

> When the LORD says, 'I am God Almighty,' He puts something into Abram, which at once changes from Abram (**אברם**) to Abraham (**אברהם**). What He adds is the letter He, ה, the chief letter of His own name 'Jehovah,' or Yahweh (**יהוה**) that sound which can only be uttered by an outbreathing—thus giving to the elect something of His own nature, (for name denotes nature,) and so by the communication of Himself and of His outbreath or spirit, molding His creature to His own pleasure, that he may be a channel of blessing to many others (emphasis and Hebrew added to provide a visual).[1]

Additionally, in verse 15, the LORD changes Sarai's name ( **שרי** ) to Sarah (**שרה**). Do you see a portion of His covenant name inserted?

8) Now, look at Abraham's response to the news about Sarah (in verses 15–16). Record how he responds and what he says, "in his heart" (v. 17).

9) What is Abraham's plan, according to verse 18?

Do you see where our flesh always has an alternate plan to God's?

10) How does God respond (v. 19 and 21)?

1 Kay Arthur, *LORD, I Want to Know You* (Colorado Springs, CO.: WaterBrook Press, 1992), 39.

Can you see that God's plan will not be altered by anyone or anything? The same is true today.

7. Now, having examined Genesis 17, let's make some connections in the chapter before we attempt to connect it to Naomi's comments to the women in Bethlehem.

   a. First, let's think about what the name God Almighty implies? In other words, what attribute or characteristic about God would best be associated with this name?

   b. Now reason with me, what is the significance of God's timing and revelation as God Almighty at this particular time when Sarah will be 90 and Abraham 100 when Isaac is born? Explain your answer.

You see, their new names now correspond with what *El Shaddai* was about to accomplish in and through their lives. In other words, *El Shaddai* (God Almighty) was about to turn an impossible, dead situation into a reality of new life! And although Sarah and Abraham laughed at God, God, Almighty, by naming the promised child Isaac, which means laughter, will have the last laugh! In other words, in reference to the life of Isaac, only God will receive the glory for his birth.

8. So, what does this have to do with Naomi and her situation? Any correlations as to why she would use the name God Almighty with the name LORD? As you begin to reason the Scriptures, think about her current situation at the end of Chapter 1.

9. Now let's look at the phrases she uses to describe her situation. First, the phrase, "the Almighty has dealt very bitterly with me." Has anyone else in the Scripture said or felt this way before?

   a. Read Job 27:2. Contextually, Job's three friends have all "counseled" Job. In his final response to his friends and their counsel, in verse 2, what does Job say? To whom does he place responsibility for his state (after death entered, with the loss of his ten children, all he possessed, and his health)?

Did you see that Job and Naomi are saying the exact thing. Did you notice their reference to the Almighty? Do you see the commonality between Job and Naomi? Have you ever felt, in some measure, like them?

10. Next, do Naomi's words sound familiar when she declares, "I went out full, but the LORD has brought me back empty" (v. 21)?

Let's look at a similar story Jesus told of another who would have said, "I went out full, but the LORD has brought me back empty." Read Luke 15:11–32, and although not the same narrative, record the undeniable similarities below.

Did you notice how the son left his father and his father's house as he went to a distant country? Did you see what the LORD used to bring the son "to his senses" (vv. 14, 17) after having attached himself to the citizens in that country (v. 15)? And did you see the father's response when his son returned? Do you think the Father responded the same way when Naomi's returned?

When a wayward one does return, does your response look more like the father or the older son? How would you want others to respond if you were the "wayward one"?

Now, consider Dr. Block's comments regarding Naomi's two statements in verse 21.

> The careful reader will notice that both statements are double-edged. On the one hand, if 'fulness' is understood in terms of food and satisfied stomachs, the first statement is patently false. Otherwise, why had they left the land of Israel in the first place? On the other hand, if 'fulness' is understood in terms of family and progeny, the statement is true. When she left, she was secure in her husband, and her future was secured by her two sons. But now she has neither, and this is what evokes the second statement.[1]

11. And finally, let's consider Naomi's rhetorical question to the women in Bethlehem, "Why do you call me Naomi, since the LORD has witnessed against me and the Almighty has afflicted me?" And earlier, she instructed the women, "Do not call me Naomi; call me Mara (which means bitter) (v. 20)? What do you see in her comments? What's going on in her heart? Now, think about her actions. Do her words and actions match? Thoughts?

Notice that Naomi was left feeling "empty" and "embittered" toward God when death entered. She did not deny or try to hide these things. Just mentioning her name, Naomi (or pleasant), caused her heart to spew. It's like Naomi can only see was His providence, but she cannot see His grace. Ever been there?

If you have ever encountered death personally, particularly in the death of a spouse or a child, or worse, "all the above," you know precisely how Naomi feels. And death can take many forms, like the loss of a marriage, a friendship, a job, a desire, or a really "good" plan. Grief can be all-consuming. When death enters a situation, it wants to reign. It wants to embitter your soul, causing everyone around you to be affected and take notice. Ultimately, its desire is for you; the last thing it wants is for you to turn to Life. And what's even harder and far more painful to reconcile in your heart is that the God you love and serve was the cause of it all. Notice I said "cause" and not the source so as not to assign the existence of evil to Him.

1 Block, *The New American Commentary: Judges/Ruth*, pp. 646–647.

But what is most important and even more telling than how she feels is where she turned and to whom did she go? Her words revealed the condition of her heart—broken and embittered, but her actions revealed what she truly believed. Her heart desperately needed a Savior, and her greatest need was for the Bread of Life. (John 6:35). She would not find Him in Moab, so, in the lovingkindness of the LORD, He was bringing her back—to Himself. Turning toward God in times of tragedy and loss is a sure sign of God's presence because it will never align with how you feel apart from Him. Can you identify?

Consider the words of the late author and biblical counselor, David Powlison, as he describes the necessity and purpose of affliction. He explains, "Affliction is where God develops you as a person so that your trust and your love come into fruition. His afflictions—and yours are the door through which God's love enters. His afflictions disciple him [Him]—and yours disciple you—into compassion for others."[1]

12. How did His afflictions disciple Him? Look at Hebrews 5:8 to discover what He, as man, learned and how He learned it.

Did you catch Powlison's phrase that affliction is the "door through which God's love enters"? Have you ever seen affliction as a door? I'm pretty sure Naomi did not, at least not yet. What she is describing seems like anything but the love of God.

Can you picture it?

There is a Latin saying that bears repeating here, which says, "*Post Tenebras Lux*," which simply means, "After darkness, Light"[2]

13. Can you think of Another in Scripture who not only lived out the phrase "*Post Tenebras Lux*" but actually became the door? Read John 10:7 to answer the question.

Could there be any greater demonstration of the love of God?

Always remember when assessing any affliction, the LORD has allowed and is using in your life, it is the necessary means to Him. And it will never be more than He was afflicted so you and I could come through the door and find eternal life.

---

1 David Powlison, *Take Heart: Daily Devotions to Deepen Your Faith* (Greensboro, NC.: New Growth Press, 2022), 88.
2 *Ibid.*, v.

14. Now, record any other thoughts, comments, or lingering questions you may still have concerning Scene Four in the space provided.

15. As you review the lesson up to this point, with whose life does your life resonate most and why?

16. And finally, do you understand why this lesson is entitled "God's Providence and Man's Choices"? How are both clearly visible? Record your observations.

**Some Concluding Thoughts to Consider:**

The following excerpts were taken from Pastor Colin Smith teaching from this portion of Scripture from the Book of Ruth:[1]

"Bitterness lurks at sorrow's door. When there is trauma, sorrow, and loss, seeds of bitterness will blow in the ground." Pastor Smith's overarching question, "Was Naomi bitter or was her experience bitter?" is telling. The way you answer this question will determine how you interpret the rest of the story.

One helpful hint to consider as you ponder his question is another question—"Where and to Whom did she turn?" Keep these things in mind as you proceed.

In addition, in the study and through the rest of the story, Orpah will not be mentioned again. Sadly, there is no mention of her in Scripture ever again. However, Ruth's story is just beginning.

1 Colin Smith, "Ruth: Ordinary People Extraordinary God," [online]; accessed September 12, 2023; available at available at https://www.youtube.com/watch?v=US50SBsr7MY; Internet. I highly recommend this entire series on Ruth by Colin Smith. You may access the entire series at https://openthebible.com. Be sure and click on the sermons by series.

# Notes

# Lesson 3

## The Lord's Provision and Protection: Man's Need

RUTH 1:22—2::23

In our last lesson, we saw everyone in the story turning, beginning with Elimelech, who turned from the "house of bread" to Moab for help. It's telling—in fact, it's instructive—that Elimelech, while seemingly turning from God's provision, care, and people to find life (bread), found death instead.

You will also recall that what at first for Elimelech was a temporary (sojourn) solution became more permanent, at least for a time, until death entered. And isn't that true with us as well? What, at first, may be a temporary solution as we attempt in our flesh to fix our problems (away from God and His people) will always result in taking us farther than we wanted to go, keeping us longer than we anticipated, and costing us more than we ever thought we'd pay.

And then we discovered after death entered, Naomi turned, except this time, she turned back to the Source of life. In Naomi's turning, Ruth and Orpah also turned at the crossroads between Moab and Bethlehem. In fact, three women left Moab: one in need of revival and two in need of regeneration. And in repentance and rest, Naomi and Ruth will be saved. However, Orpah proved unwilling (see Isaiah 30:15). One turned back to her God, one turned from her idols to serve the living God, and one turned entirely away from God back to her idols.

You see, death, as many of you may personally know, has a way of becoming the furnace of affliction whereby those who belong to the Lord are severely tested and tried. And those who are His will eventually turn to Him rather than away from Him, knowing He is the only hope and source of bread (life). And those who do not belong to Him will eventually turn away, proving they never were.

Clearly, from Scripture, the LORD uses the afflictions in life, such as the fiery furnace of death, to expose and reveal what is in our hearts. Once tested and tried, the believer, like the psalmist, will joyfully say, "It was good for me that I was afflicted, so that I may learn Your statutes" (Ps. 119:71).

So, as we begin this lesson, and until the end of the book, we will examine what it looks like to be brought back into the "house of bread" as God's providence unfolds His restoration plan.

Are you ready to get started?

## Days One and Two

### Scene Five: Putting the Pieces Together in 1:22—2:7

1. Begin today's lesson with prayer.

2. Read the fifth scene of the narrative, which takes place in Ruth 1:22–2:7 and record the people, places, and events in this section below.

I. Who are the people in these verses? List them in the order they occur in the story. (Consider including the verse numbers.)

Next, record the significant place in Scene Five.

II. What places are mentioned in this section? Keep in mind any reference to time fits in here.

III. Now, beginning with Ruth 1:22, briefly list the events in this scene as they occurred. Consider including the verse numbers.

**Gathering Information**

Note: The barley and wheat harvest lasted seven weeks and culminated in celebrating the Feast of Weeks (see Deut. 16:9–12). On our calendar, the barley (grain) harvest would begin in mid-to-late April and last until the first week of June. [Some references listed late March to late May or early June, depending on when the seed was planted months prior.]

Now, note that there are three Hebrew words that will be used interchangeably in the narrative that describe Boaz's relation specifically to Elimelech and therefore, Naomi, that when translated in English, appear to be the same word but they are not.

The first Hebrew word in the narrative is *moda*, a noun meaning "kindred, relative."[1] It is used in Ruth 2:1, and 3:2. It is a more general term than *goel*.

The second word is the adjective *qarob*, used figuratively (closely related to *moda*), which indicates a relationship, a relative among humans, but also a relationship to God.[2] It is used in Ruth 2:20, and translated, "our relative."

The third Hebrew word, *goel* or *ga'al*, is "a verb meaning to redeem or act as a kinsman-redeemer; to reclaim as one's own. The word means to act as a redeemer for a deceased kinsman (Ruth 3:13); to redeem or buy back a kinsman's possessions (Lev. 25:26); to avenge a kinsman's murder (Num. 35:19); to redeem an object through a payment (Lev. 27:13). Theologically, this word is used to convey God's redemption of individuals from spiritual death and His redemption of the nation of Israel from Egyptian bondage and also from exile (Ex. 6:6)."[3]

It is used in Ruth 2:20: 3:9, 12 (2 times), 13 (4 times); 4:1, 3, 6, 8, 14. Furthermore, *goel* is translated, "redeem" in Ruth 4:4 (5 times), 6 (2 times), and "redemption" in Ruth 4:6–7.

As you look at the repetition, can you see the central theme in the narrative is redemption?

Note: Boaz is described in Ruth 2:1 as a "man of great wealth" in the NASB, and the ESV uses the term "worthy." The actual Hebrew word used, *gibbor*, is an adjective meaning "strong, mighty."[4]

Now, note the word *favor* used in Ruth 2:2, 10, and 13 is the Hebrew word *hen*, which, when translated, means grace, unmerited (unearned) favor, and it "conveys a sense of acceptance and preference."[5]

Note: In the last lesson, we gathered information regarding the levirate marriage from Deuteronomy 25:5–10, so that the name of the deceased would continue, but in this lesson, we will add the redemption of land found in Leviticus 25:23–25.

1. Read Leviticus 25:23–25 and record the facts concerning the redemption of land.

Further reading in Leviticus 25:26–28 concerns the man with no kinsman from which to redeem the land. Did you notice in Leviticus 25:23–28, the key word, "man"? The exact wording is significant according to ancient Eastern customs; women were prohibited by husbands from owning or inheriting property, even upon their husbands' death. When you understand this concept, you can see the actual state of poverty and destitution in which Naomi found herself.

But what about the daily care of the widow? Was there any provision for them? How would they eat? Where could they find daily bread?

2. Look at the following cross-references, which concern the law of gleaning, (also a picture of His grace), and record your observations. Be sure to include the provision itself, who it was for, and the Source of the provision allotted.

1 Baker and Carpenter, *The Complete Word Study Dictionary Old Testament*, 579.
2 *Ibid.*, 1013.
3 *Ibid.*, 176.
4 Francis Brown, C.A. Briggs, and S.R. Driver, (*Enhanced Brown-Driver-Briggs Hebrew and English Lexicon* (Oxford, England: Clarendon Press, 1977), 150, accessed April, 7, 2023: Logos Bible Software edition.
5 Baker and Carpenter, *The Complete Word Study Dictionary Old Testament*, 354.

a. Leviticus 19:9–10 –

b. Leviticus 23:22 –

c. Deuteronomy 24:19–22

So, what else did the LORD say concerning the widow? Often, you will see the fatherless (orphan) intricately linked together in Scripture, for these were considered the most vulnerable, weak, and poor in society in ancient Eastern culture.

3. Look at some other Scriptures regarding the care of widows and the fatherless. Read the cross-references and record the facts about them in the space provided.

   a. Exodus 22:22–24 –

   b. Deuteronomy 10:18

   c. Deuteronomy 24:17–18 –

   d. Psalm 68:5 –

The ESV uses the word, "Protector" for the widow. I like that best!

   e. Psalm 82:3 - ____________________________________________________

f. Psalm 146:9 - ____________________________________________________

g. Proverbs 23:10–11 –

h. Isaiah 1:17 –

i. Jeremiah 7: (5) 6–7 –

When you read verse 5, what does it imply? Were they obediently taking care of the aliens, widows, and orphans?

j. Now, read Malachi 3:5. Record the company that oppressors of the widows, orphans, and aliens keep in the eyes of the LORD.

1) What will they all incur? ________________________________

Eye-opening, isn't it? Malachi 3:5 puts the care of aliens, widows, and orphans in God's perspective, doesn't it?

k. Now read James 1:27 and record what the Scriptures call "pure and undefiled religion in the sight of God and Father."

4. As you consider all the cross-references above, what do you see about the Character/Person and Word of the LORD regarding the widow and the fatherless?

And finally, as you study the next portion of Scripture you need to see the distinction between the reapers and the gleaners.

Note: The word "reapers" (*qasar*) refers to those who were hired to gather the crop. In other words, they had a right to be in the field and, in essence, belonged. It is used figuratively of those who "reap a harvest or the fruit of righteousness" (Hos. 10:12); and of evil (Hos. 8:7).[1]

However, the verb glean (*laqat*) means to pick up and gather the leftovers from the corners of the field to make provision for the gleaners who were the needy, the widow, the orphan, and the foreigner. Interestingly, the same word is used in Exodus 16:4 in reference to manna, the bread from heaven sent by God to provide and sustain the lives of His people while in the wilderness.[2]

Please pay close attention to these two words and the order in which they are used. And to help, keep in mind Ruth the Moabitess will never be referred to as a reaper in the story, and there is a clear distinction. As the story progresses, pay attention to how Ruth is referred to in each verse.

Keep all this information in mind as you continue to put the pieces together. In each of the following scenes, you will see separate conversations. Also, remember the literary tools of repetition and the split-screen technique discussed earlier. Consider what is being said and who says it as the story continues to unfold.

**Putting the Pieces Together**

1. First, compare Ruth 1:1 and 1:22. Record the various contrasts from the beginning (v. 1) to the end of the chapter (v. 22). What do you see?

2. Considering the contrasts above, what is the difference maker? You will find the answer between the verses (vv. 2–21). You could also answer with one key repeated word. Do you remember it? ____________________________

3. Now, let's look at the transition from Ruth 1:22 to 2:1. As you think about the literary tools of repetition and the split-screen technique, what do you see? Think about the description of each person as you answer. You should see a contrast between Naomi and Ruth in verse 22 and the introduction of Boaz in Ruth 2:1.

1 Baker and Carpenter, *The Complete Word Study Dictionary Old Testament*, pp. 1008–1009.
2 *Ibid.*, 555.

Now, from Ruth 2:2–7 there will be three separate conversations recorded, one at home and two in the field, outlined as follows:

Verse 2: Ruth the Moabitess and Naomi

Verse 4: Boaz and the Reapers

Verses 5–7: Boaz and his servant in charge

4. As you consider the conversations record your insights below. Think carefully about the words used, the questions asked, and the descriptions the narrator chose to record. What do you see?

5. Once again, remembering the literary tools of repetition and the split–screen technique, evaluate Ruth 2:3, where the narrator speaks into the story. Include whom he wants you to see. Record your observations.

6. Now, as you think about the mundane everyday work Ruth was willing to do in verse 2 and consider how the narrator speaks into the events in verse 3, what do you see about the providence of God working His redemptive plan as Ruth did her mundane tasks? How does Ruth's work ethic speak into the mundane of your everyday life? Read Psalm 37:23–24 as you process the question. Thoughts?

As I think of both Naomi and Ruth's situation, I am reminded of something Elisabeth Elliot said when her husband, Jim Elliot, along with four other missionaries, was speared to death for attempting to take the gospel to the uncivilized cannibals known as the Auca/Waodani tribe. When asked how she made it alone in the jungle with her ten-month-old daughter, she said she survived by doing the next thing.

With death, grief, poverty, and hunger looming, Ruth did the next thing. What about you? Can you identify with Naomi or Ruth? Could the mundane things in your life be providence leading and directing your steps (see Psalm 37:23–24)? Are you willing to let Him lead you to Himself?

7. Next, let's look at *how* Boaz greets the reapers working for him and how they respond. Typically, the greeting for a fellow Israelite would have been, "shalom," which is a greeting of peace. Notice, however, the wording used and compare it with Numbers 6:24–26. Do you see any similarities? Record your insights below.

a. What does such a greeting imply between Boaz and his reapers?

8. Now, look again at verses 2–7 but this time, focus on the distinction between the gleaner and the reaper. Record your insights below as you keep in mind the reapers were hired workers and had every right to be in the field. Gleaners, on the other hand, were in the "field of grace" because of the LORD'S provision. To help you think through this portion, read Romans 1:16b to see the distinction and God's order.

a. Considering these insights, look at Matthew 15:21–28 and record the parallels between Jesus's conversation with a Canaanite woman. Any similarities? Pay close attention and record what the Lord Jesus saw and responded to in the woman. In other words, is Jesus looking at her through a physical or spiritual lens?

9. Next, in Ruth 2:5–6, notice what Boaz asks his servant in charge. Notice he doesn't ask, "Who is she?" but rather, "Whose young woman is this?" What does Boaz want to know? And then think about how the servant interprets the question. Notice what he focuses and calls attention to in his response. In other words, what does the servant in charge see? (v. 6). Finally, is Boaz put off by the servant's answer? In other words, what does Boaz see? To help you think through these questions, consider Boaz's lineage, particularly his mother. Lots to consider as you process. Any thoughts?

## Day Three

### Scene Six: Putting the Pieces Together in Ruth 2:8–13

1. Begin today's lesson with prayer.
2. Read the sixth scene of the narrative, which takes place in Ruth 2:8–13 and record the people, places, and events in this section below.

I. Who are the people in these verses? List them in the order they occur in the story. (Consider including the verse numbers.)

Next, record the significant place in the sixth scene.

II. What places are mentioned in this section? Also, keep in mind any reference to time.

III. Now, beginning with Ruth 2:8, briefly list the events in this scene as they occurred. Notice the various conversations, and when the narrator adds information.

**Gathering Information**

As you may have noticed, this scene records Boaz and Ruth's first encounter and subsequent conversations. There is nothing new to gather, only reminders.

The word "favor" (*hen*) means grace (vv. 10, 13). And in verse 13, the term "kindly" is the Hebrew word *hesed*, translated lovingkindness, as discussed in our previous lesson. Keep in mind, these are both attributes of God, not man.

Remember the distinction between the gleaner and the reaper and think about what both represent as the story continues to unfold.

**Putting the Pieces Together**

1. Let's begin by examining what Boaz told Ruth in verses 8–9. Notice how he begins his instruction and what he calls her (the same as Naomi in verse 2). To help interpret, consider the following words and their meanings. Record your observations in the space provided.

**Note:** The word translated as "listen carefully" is one Hebrew word. It is the same word used at the beginning of the *Shema*, in Deuteronomy 6:4, which states, "Hear, O Israel!" (emphasis added). The word *Shema* means to heed, listen, and obey. The Shema was a prayer recited twice a day (morning and evening) by every devout Jew, acknowledging that Yahweh alone was God. Notice it is addressed to God's people.

Additionally, the term "eyes" in verse 9 refers to either one's physical lens or the Source. Remember, think "split-screen" when interpreting.

2. If you had to summarize what Boaz is offering Ruth in two words, what do you see?

a. ________________________________

and

b. ________________________________

Does that remind you of anyone?

3. Next, let's look at Ruth's response in verse 10. What is she doing and saying? Thoughts?

4. Now, let's focus on Boaz' reply to Ruth in verses 12–13. These verses are packed with theology.

   a. First, let's address what Boaz says about Ruth in verse 12. What does Boaz recognize in Ruth? Look at Genesis 12:1–3 and record any similarities when the LORD called him out of Ur. Keep in mind how Scripture always connects Abraham with faith and then think about what Jesus saw in the Canaanite woman in Matthew 15:21–28.

Do you think Boaz saw God at work in the life of Ruth, just as Jesus saw the Father at work in the Gentile woman and joined Him?

b. Now compare the things Boaz recognized in Ruth with what Jesus said to His disciples in Mark 10:29–30. What do you see?

c. Next, let's focus on what Boaz says about the LORD (v. 12). What do you learn about the specific name of God to which Boaz refers, and how does that tie in with Ruth's provision and protection?

d. As you consider the phrase "under whose wings you have come to seek refuge," does your mind go to the Psalms, where this kind of figurative language is used in the description of God? Interestingly, Moses, the author of Psalm 91, uses the same terminology. Record your insights.

1) Psalm 91:4 -

2) Now let's pause here so you can read the entire psalm today. Will you allow God's Spirit to minister to you if your heart needs refuge? The Savior is waiting. Record your insights below.

**Rhetorical Question:** Knowing Psalm 91 came from Moses, what does that tell you about Boaz, his parents, and their relationship with God's Word? And how should that instruct you regarding your children and grandchildren?

e. Look at Proverbs 30:5. What do you see?

f. Now, look at several cross-references in the Psalms written by David about the LORD, our refuge. Taking a few, read Psalm 16:1; 18:1–2, and 30; 31:1, 19; 34:8, 22; 59:16; 62:7; 118:8, and record below some of the words and phrases associated with the LORD, our refuge.

1) As you consider that these truths were passed down *to* David, can you trace the human instruments used? To answer, see Ruth 4:21–22.

Again, do you see the importance of God's Word in your life? Generations from now, your life, words, and teaching will matter! Who knows, there may be a Spurgeon in your family line right now.

5. Now, look at Ruth's response to Boaz in verse 13. What does she recognize in him and his actions? Think about the words she uses and the Source of each as you answer.

6. Now, compare Ruth 2:13 with Ruth 1:8. What do you see? Look at the words used to help answer.

7. Any additional insights you may have from Ruth 2:8–13 can be added here.

## Day Four

### Scene Seven: Putting the Pieces Together in Ruth 2:14–16

1. Begin today's lesson with prayer.

2. Today's lesson will cover the seventh scene in Ruth 2:14–16. Start by recording the people, places, and events in this section below.

I. Who are the people in these verses? List them in the order they occur in the story. (Consider including the verse numbers.)

Next, record the significant place in the seventh scene.

II. What places are mentioned in this section? Also, keep in mind any reference to time.

III. Now, beginning with Ruth 2:14, briefly list the events in this scene as they occurred. Notice the various conversations, and when the narrator adds information.

**Gathering Information:** In this scene and the next (Scene 8), one of the truths to focus upon is the term "satisfied." In this scene, the Hebrew verb *saba* is translated "satisfied" and means "to have had enough of something or too much."[1] Even more telling is how the word is used in Scripture. Let's look at a couple.

1. Look at Exodus 16:8 and 12, where this same word is used and translated, "full" and "filled," respectively. Record who, what, when, where, how, and why this word is used.

2. Read Deuteronomy 6:10–11. What do you see here?

**Putting the Pieces Together**

1. Let's begin with verse 14 in Ruth 2. Notice the mealtime and the invitation to "Come." Notice Ruth's position to the reapers. Also look closely at who served whom? What comes to mind?

Did you catch that this little Moabitess has been given a place at the table or in the meal with Boaz and the harvesters? Do you know of any meal where the Jew and Gentile will sit side by side to be served by their Master?

2. Let's pause here to look at a couple of passages that may help shed light on what the meal, the gathering and placement of both Jew and Gentile together, and the Master serving until each is satisfied represent. Read the references and then compile a list of similarities.

   a. Matthew 22:1–14

   b. Revelation 19:7–9

1 Baker and Carpenter, *The Complete Word Study Dictionary Old Testament*, 1094.

3. Now, as you compare Ruth being "satisfied" (v.14) with the Exodus and Deuteronomy cross-references, do you see a common Source and thread? Thoughts?

4. Now, compare Ruth's satisfied state with leftovers (v. 14) with John 6:114. Record your insights and the similarities (for there are several).

5. Notice in this scene that Boaz has two conversations, one with Ruth and immediately afterward with his servants. Record any additional insights from these two conversations not already covered. Again, think about how the reapers would have viewed the gleaner, hence, Boaz's instructions throughout the narrative.

*Do you see the LORD'S lavish gifts of place, provision, and protection?*

## Day Five

### Scene Eight: Putting the Pieces Together in Ruth 2:17–23

Finally, as we transition to the story's eighth and final scene in chapter 2, record the people, places, and events in Ruth 2:17–23 on the next page.

I. Who are the people in these verses? List them in the order they occur in the story. (Consider including the verse numbers.)

Next, record the significant place in the eighth scene.

II. What places are mentioned in this section? Also, keep in mind any reference

III. Now, beginning with Ruth 2:17–23, briefly list the events in this scene as they occurred. Notice the various conversations, and when the narrator adds information.

**Gathering Information:**

**Note:** Although the dry measurement weight of an ephah is uncertain, Old Testament professor, Daniel Block cites Jewish historian Josephus, who records its measurement equivalent to the *bath*, which was thirty-six liters. Additionally, Block explains,

> To thresh an ephah of grain from one day's labor is an extraordinary feat, not to mention Ruth's having to carry it home! Depending upon the quality of the grain and which standard one uses, an ephah of barley could have weighed from thirty to fifty pounds.[1]

In the previous scene, you will recall the word "satisfied." However, instead of the verb *saba* used in scene 7 describing Ruth, the noun *soba* is used in this section about Naomi. And as you already know, a noun defines existence.

The use of this noun is directly linked with Israel's obedience and God's blessing in Leviticus 26:5 and Deuteronomy 23:24–25. It is used figuratively of the fullness of joy (Ps. 16:11) and the fullness of food that God gave the Israelites in the wilderness (Ps. 78:25). And in Proverbs 13:25, we learn the righteous will have enough and more to meet their needs.[2]

**Putting the Pieces Together**

1. As you read verses 17 and 18, the narrator gives us some amazing insights. Again, keep in mind anything repetitive and any display of the split-screen technique. What do you see?

1 Block, *Judges, Ruth* Vol. 6, 670, accessed April 8, 2023: Logos Bible Software edition.

2 Baker and Carpenter, *The Complete Word Study Dictionary Old Testament*, 1094.

2. Next, let's focus on the conversation between Naomi and Ruth in verses 19–22.

   a. Begin with the first phrase, "May he who took notice of you be blessed" (v. 19). The term "take notice" is a Hebrew word used in the causative stem, meaning the subject is actively the cause. With that knowledge, do you see two perspectives from the split-screen technique? Explain.

   b. Next, address what Naomi says about the LORD in verse 20. Notice the word "kindness" or the Hebrew equivalent, *hesed* is used here. Record your insights below.

   c. Also, in verse 20, two Hebrew words are used to describe Boaz. First, the word *qarob* is translated as "our relative," and second, *goel* translates as "our closest relative." By using these terms as they appear in verse 20, what is Naomi beginning to see, and how does that tie in with her acknowledgment of the LORD?

3. How does Ruth 2:20 compare with Naomi's prayer in Ruth 1:8?

4. Record any other insights gleaned from the narrator's comments and the conversation between Naomi and Ruth in verses 17–22 in the space provided. Do not feel pressured to fill in all the blank spaces; they are merely provided if needed.

5. Now, let's look at the narrator's summary statement in verse 23. Any insights to record?

6. As you think about the timing of the barley and wheat harvests mentioned, about how long has Ruth gleaned? What does that tell you about Ruth, the LORD, and work?

Always remember, the concept of work originated Pre-Fall; therefore, it is a good gift from the LORD. What does that tell you about people who refuse to work? Just a thought.

7. Now, look back over verses 17–23 and pick out Ruth and every verb associated with her. Do you see an abbreviated story?

8. As we bring this lesson to a close, look back over Ruth 2, specifically noting words like favor (*grace*) and kindness (*hesed*), which are attributes of the LORD, not man. Also, think about the name *Yahweh* (LORD) as you understand its meaning from previous lessons and consider God's providence (purposeful acts) in chapter 2 of Ruth. What do you see about the LORD, our God?

9. Now, think about the people, places, and events of your life this week. Could this same LORD be providentially at work in your life right now? Take some time to prayerfully record anything the Spirit brings to mind. It would be such a shame to miss Him this week.

10. Now, look at the title of the lesson. After having completed the lesson do you agree with the title, or do you have a better one? Explain.

In our next lesson, we will look at chapter 3 of Ruth. Prepare to be challenged and required to pray much and ponder deeply.

# Notes

# Lesson 4

## The Lord's Plan Will Not Be Thwarted by Man's Plan

RUTH 3:1–18

In the last chapter, we saw the LORD, in His lovingkindness (*hesed*) and favor or grace (*hen*), provide for the poor, the widow, and the foreigner in ways only God's providence could. And by looking into the lives of Naomi and Ruth, we discover that our lives run parallel, for apart from the LORD'S lovingkindness and grace, we too represent the poor, the widow, the foreigner, and the orphan.

As we head into chapter three, we find ourselves in controversial territory, for the analysis of the events in this chapter are as diverse as the theologian interpreting. And so, we tread lightly and pray much as we wade through what appears, murky waters.

Are you ready to get started?

### Day One

### Scene Nine: Putting the Pieces Together in Ruth 3:1–5

As always, begin today's lesson with prayer.

Read the ninth scene of the narrative, Ruth 3:1–5 and record the people, places, and events in this section below.

1. Who are the people in these verses? List them in the order they occur in the story. (Consider including the verse numbers.)

Next, record the significant place in scene nine.

II. What place(s) is mentioned in this section?

III. Now, beginning with verse 1, briefly list the events in this scene as they occurred. Consider including the verse numbers.

**Gathering Information**

Our first word to consider in the ninth scene is the term "security" (*manoah*), which means "resting place." In particular, Ruth 3:1 represents "a time or place of security."[1] The same word is used figuratively in Psalm 116:7. Because cross-references help us define the word more clearly, look at this psalm and the verses surrounding the use of the term.

1. Read Psalm 116:5–9 and answer the following questions:

   a. Record what is specifically secure (or at rest)? ___________________________

Do you see who is specifically connected to the rest and security our soul needs?

   b. What are the LORD'S attributes and actions associated with this security?

Now, before we proceed, look back at Ruth 1:9, where a related word is used. You will recognize this as Naomi's prayer for her daughters-in-law at the crossroads between Moab and Bethlehem. Here, she petitions the LORD for rest (Heb. *menuhah*), which "denotes places where peace, quiet, and trust are present."[2] Also keep in mind that geographical places can have spiritual connotations attached.

Next, the word Naomi uses for "kinsman" in verse 2 is the Hebrew term *moda*. As you may recall, this word is used for a distant relative. However, the more specific term Ruth uses with Boaz in verse 9 is *goel*.

To help us better understand the word *goel* as it compares to the more general term, *moda*, consider the following from the late evangelist and Bible teacher Roy Hession, who explains three conditions necessary to qualify as kinsman redeemer (*goel*):

1 Baker and Carpenter, *The Complete Word Study Dictionary Old Testament*, 627.
2 Ibid., 628.

- ☐ He had to be a family member
- ☐ He had to have the power and ability (i.e., financially) to redeem
- ☐ He had to be willing

Moreover, all three things were necessary. In other words, you couldn't just be a family member with the power to redeem if you were unwilling. Or if you had the means and were willing but not a family member, you would not qualify. Keep these things in mind while interpreting this scene and the next (vv. 6–13).

Also noteworthy, in verse 3, under the specific instructions given to meet Boaz, the phrase, "put on your best clothes" in the NASB, is not as accurate as the ESV, which reads, "put on your cloak," because the "cloak" was an outer garment that could serve two purposes, a coat, and a blanket, especially for the poor (see. Ex. 22:25–26).

Next, we must address the controversial parts of the chapter. In this scene, Naomi gives Ruth counsel. Some interpreters would say Naomi took matters into her own hands and developed a dangerous scheme that could have quickly backfired.

Naomi's instruction to "uncover his feet and lie down" can be taken two completely different ways. One view takes the phrase literally, and the other view factors in a figure of speech. For example, the Hebrew word "to uncover" can be considered a euphemism, meaning one's genitals or skirt. So, whether you read Naomi's instructions literally or interpret them using a figure of speech, these issues must be considered as you analyze the passage.

Suffice it to say one interpretation factors in the flesh (helping God out, as if He needs our help), and the other view factors in a display of God's Spirit (by trusting Him and His Word). Do you see how the position you lean toward will bias Naomi's instruction and Ruth's actions in the entire chapter?

Therefore, as you examine the scenario in verses 1–5 and 6–13, you too will have to decide, but do so prayerfully, for it will not be easy to choose. I guess you could say that in the end, you are left to decide the motive of the hearts of others, and that, as you may already know, is not biblically possible because "The heart is more deceitful than all else, and is desperately sick; who can understand it?" (Jer. 17:9). The answer rests, of course, in the LORD who alone can search it (Jer. 17:10).

Consequently, as you wrestle with the interpretation of scenes 9 and 10 (Ruth 3:1–5 and 6–13, respectively) (for you most certainly will), the pressing question is not *why* the narrator would allow us to struggle with the controversial conversations and events, but *that* he allowed us to struggle with them. And with that, we must turn to the One who knows all things.

So, now that you have been forewarned, let's get started and try to piece this all together.

**Putting the Pieces Together**

1. Let's start by comparing Naomi's first rhetorical question in Ruth 3:1 with what she asked the LORD in Ruth 1:9. What do you see? Pay careful attention to Naomi's exact wording in Ruth 3:1, "Shall I not seek security...." What is she saying to Ruth? Keep in mind what you saw in Psalm 116:7 to help. Thoughts?

**Note:** The phrase, "that it may be well with you" is attached to something specifically. For example, look at Deuteronomy 4:40; 6:17–18; and 12:28 and record the association. In other words, what must first take place "that it to go well with you"?

Do you see that when Israel kept the LORD'S commands it would go well with them? Therefore, can you see that Naomi was seeking rest in a Person and in obedience to His Word?

2. Now, for clarity, record Naomi's exact instructions in the order they occur in verses 3–4. Be specific.

3. Now, as you consider Naomi's second rhetorical question (v. 2) and the fact she knows that Boaz will be winnowing the barley at the threshing floor that night, make a list of the personal instructions using only the verbs she used in verses 3a and 4b. Notice there are 4 in each verse. See if you can align the verbs with one to two words each (because they align in the Hebrew).

v. 3a - ______________ ______________ ______________ ______________

v. 4b - ______________ ______________ ______________ ______________

Note: According to Old Testament scholar, Daniel Block, Naomi's three-fold instruction for Ruth to "wash" meant to bathe, to "anoint" is the instruction to use oil or perfume, and to "put on" her cloak, could possibly mean "that Naomi is hereby advising Ruth to end her period of mourning over her widowhood and get on with normal life."[1] He further suggests that more than likely, Ruth might have been wearing mourning clothes up to this point, which may have, inadvertently, caused Boaz to pause and not pursue out of respect.[2]

To help us think through these instructions, let's compare them with another place where the exact Hebrew words, "wash, anoint yourself, and change your clothes," were used after death.

4. Read 2 Samuel 12 for context. Notice this chapter follows David's adultery with Bathsheba and the murder of Uriah, her husband (2 Samuel 11). Focus on verse 20, where we find the exact words "washed, anointed, and changed his clothes," which are the exact same instructions Naomi gave Ruth. As you read verses 18–24, record the similarities between David's situation and outcome and Naomi and Ruth. What do you see?

1 Block, *Judges, Ruth*, Vol. 6, 684.

2 *Ibid.*

Could Naomi's instructions to Ruth be the same as David's after sin and death entered? Might Naomi be telling Ruth it's time to wash from mourning and grief, anoint herself, exchange her mourning clothes, and worship the only One who can restore life? After all, true worship involves love and obedience to the LORD and His Word.

Are you beginning to see how a close look at each instruction can be interpreted quite differently depending on the motive in which the instruction was given and the lens from which it is viewed?

Moreover, the instructions from verse 4 can be misconstrued depending on the interpretation of the wording presented. For example, Ruth is to "uncover his feet" and go and lie down herself.

To help you understand the dilemma in interpretation, allow me to share some information that may shed light as to why the controversy exists.

Again, I will defer to Dr. Block's comments on this section in Ruth as he explains,

Few texts in the book have generated as much discussion as this command. There is a line of interpretation that treats it as a command to engage in risqué and seductive behavior. It seems that in this cultural context, at winnowing time the threshing floor often became a place of illicit sexual behavior. Realizing that the men would spend the night in the fields next to the piles of grain, prostitutes would go out to them and offer their services. As a Moabite, Ruth might not have had scruples about feigning the role of a prostitute to secure a sexual favor from a "near relative" any more than Tamar did in Genesis 38.

This interpretation is rendered all the more attractive by the fact that each of the three Hebrew words that make up this sentence is capable of more than one meaning, and each is capable of bearing an overtly sexual meaning. First, the root *glh*, 'to uncover,' is often used in sexual contexts of 'uncovering someone's nakedness" (a euphemism for exposing the genitals) or of "uncovering someone's skirt." Second, the final verb, *šākab*, 'to lie,' is often used to denote sexual relations. Third, the noun between these verbs, *margĕlôt*, derives from *regel*, 'foot,' the dual and plural of which may be used euphemistically for the genitalia. Not surprisingly, therefore, some interpret Naomi's scheme as delicate and dangerous, charged with sexual overtones.[1]

Are you beginning to understand the reasoning behind the controversy? So how does one reconcile any other position? As you prayerfully weigh the facts, I suggest you consider who is saying these things and what might be her motivation—just a suggestion.

5. Now, considering all the information provided, as you read verses 1–5, and specifically Naomi's instructions to Ruth, is she plotting a scheme to trap Boaz? Is she instructing Ruth to lure Boaz somehow? In other words, in which camp of interpretation do you land? As you answer, consider what is motivating Naomi's heart. In defense of either position, as you answer, be sure to explain your position using the Scripture.

1 *Ibid.*, 685.

6. Now, what do you see in Ruth's response to Naomi's instructions (v. 5)?

I can only imagine what you're thinking as you have had to wrestle with this section in Ruth. I want to say, I completely understand. For there has been much prayer as I too have struggled with it. In the end, whatever position you take, make sure it is grounded in God's Word and not in your opinion.

As the story keeps progressing, we will look at another scenario that is equally difficult and controversial, as we attempt to interpret Ruth's actions and Boaz's response accurately.

## Days Two–Four

### Scene Ten: Putting the Pieces Together in Ruth 3:6–13

1. As always, begin today's lesson with prayer.
2. Read the tenth scene of the narrative, Ruth 3:6–13 and record the people, places, and events in this section below.

I. Who are the people in these verses? List them in the order they appear in the story. (Consider including the verse numbers.)

Next, record the significant place in scene ten.

II. What place(s) is mentioned in this section? Again, time is also a factor.

Note: Faith is deeply tested when things seem to be at their darkest.

III. Now, beginning with verse 1, briefly list the events in this scene as they occurred. Consider including the verse numbers.

**Gathering Information**

Let's begin with some information about the threshing floor. Geographically, the town of Bethlehem is situated high above sea level in mountainous terrain. Therefore, traveling away from the city would mean one would have to go down, and on any journey into the city, the traveler would have to go up.

Old Testament scholar and professor Edward F. Campbell's comments may be helpful here as we consider the concept and significance of the threshing floor. He explains,

First, a threshing floor was probably located close enough to the city gate to allow ease of carrying the grain into town and ease of keeping watch over the grain during the threshing and winnowing operations. Second, the threshing floor was probably an open space, large enough for many to thresh and winnow at the same time, which was sufficiently exposed to the prevailing west wind to take advantage of it for the winnowing process. Third, certain public occasions, especially judicial hearings, could properly be held at the threshing floor near the gate; this is the case in 1 Kings 22.[1]

Furthermore, the threshing floor represents a place of separation and revelation in Scripture. Consequently, it can have both physical and spiritual connotations. In this place, the harvest was readied by separating the grain from the chaff to reveal and gather sustenance.

1. In addition, bear in mind that it was common for someone to sleep near the grain at night so that no one could come and steal the grain or wheat. With that thought in mind, look at John 10:10. Do you see any symbolism with what's at stake as Boaz protects the seed?

Next, note in verse 7, Boaz is described as having "eaten and drunk and his heart was merry." The term for "merry," (*yatab*), means "to be good, well, pleasing" and "describes a heart that is happy."[2] Also noteworthy, in the cross-references where *yatab* is used, it is never a description of an inebriated heart.

Likewise, the word "drunk" (*satah*) is a verb that simply implies drinking as in any liquid, and only when used in the passive sense does it mean to be drunk (Lev. 11:34), which in this case, it is not in the passive sense.[3]

**Note:** The term "maid," in verse 9, is the Hebrew noun, *amah*, used figuratively to "express humility." And *goel* is the term used for "close relative" in verses 9 and 12 (2 times) and "redeem" in verse 13 (4 times) for a total of six times.

1 Edward F. Campbell, *Ruth: A New Translation with Introduction, Notes, and Commentary, Vol. 7,* (New Haven, CT: Yale University Press, 2008), 118, accessed April 15, 2023: Logos Bible Software edition.

2 Baker and Carpenter, *The Complete Word Study Dictionary Old Testament*, 445.

3 *Ibid.*, 1206.

This scene introduces us to a rather peculiar and unfamiliar phrase when Ruth says, "spread your covering over your maid" (v. 9). The word "covering" (*kanap*) used here is the same Hebrew word Boaz used describing Ruth's relationship to the LORD in 2:12. It can be translated as "wing, the skirt or corner of a garment."[1] Here it is used as an idiom and means "to take to wife."[2] The vocabulary could also suggest a request for immediate relations or a marriage invitation. Again, the motive of the heart and Ruth's character must be considered when interpreting.

2. Now, consider another place the word *kanap* is used, except this time, the LORD is the One saying it. Read Ezekiel 16:8 and record your observations. What is the LORD saying, and how is He using the word? [For context, you may read verses 1–14, where the LORD expounds on His election (choice) and covenant (agreement) with Israel as a nation.]

Keep this in mind as you start to put the pieces together in the next section.

Note: The word "excellence" in Boaz's description of Ruth (v. 11) means "strength and influence."[3]

**Putting the Pieces Together**

1. As you read verse 6, what are your thoughts concerning the phrase, "she went down to the threshing floor"? Consider the narrator's choice of words and the interplay in the spiritual realm. Keep in mind the information provided earlier as you consider what is happening. Also, remember that this scene could have played out anywhere and at any time, as you answer.

Consider the visual of a typical threshing floor.[4]

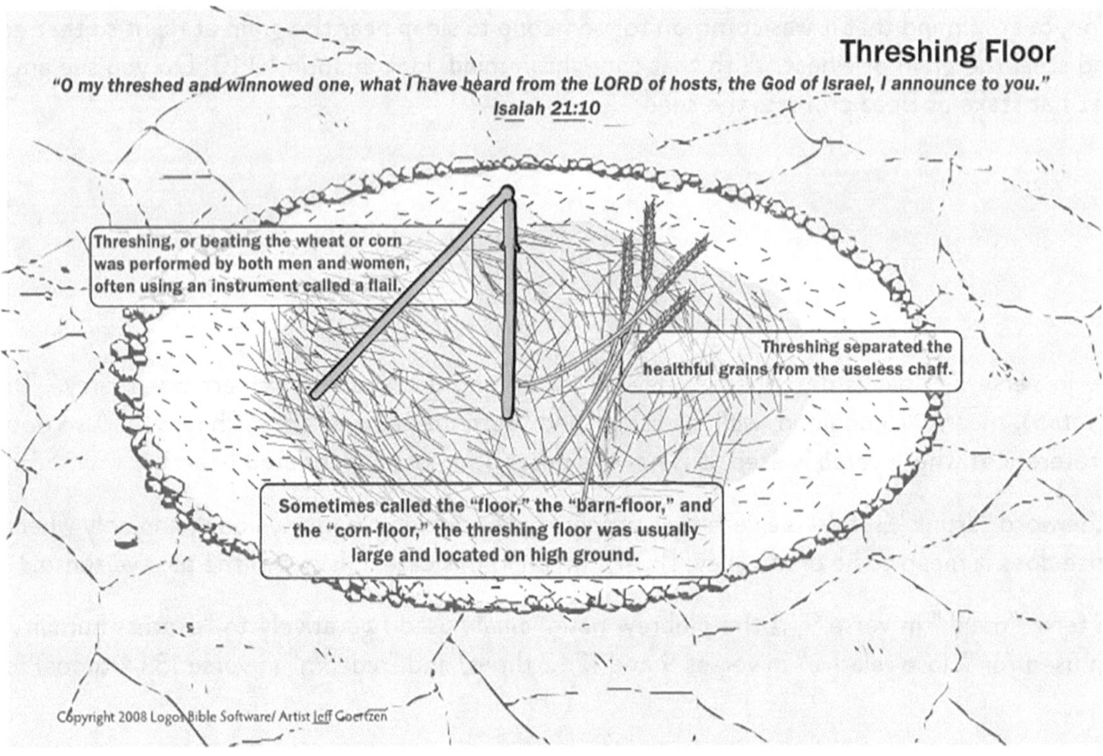


1 *Ibid.*, 514.
2 *Ibid.*
3 Baker and Carpenter, *The Complete Word Study Dictionary Old Testament*, 334.
4. Threshing Floor diagram courtesy of Logos Bible Software, a division of Faithlife Corporation. Used by permission.

Could the journey downward represent a place of humility as Ruth obeys?

2. Now, consider verse 7 and the wording used as you compare and contrast this scenario with one previously examined in Genesis 19:32–38. The plan and this scene, in particular, appear eerily familiar, doesn't it?

In fact, the words "lie/lay/lying down" (*sakab*) used in Genesis 19:32, 33 (2 times), 34, and 35 (2 times) is the same word used in Ruth 3:4 (3 times), v. 7 (2 times), and verses 8, 13, and 14.

By definition, *sakab* means to lie down physically or sleep, but it also assumes and implies the resting posture or being at rest. In addition, it can be used figuratively as well, as with Lot's daughters. It is also a euphemism for death (see Gen. 47:30; Job 3:13). Strikingly, it is also used figuratively to describe the LORD'S betrothing of Israel to Himself (Hos. 2:18 [20]).

So, as you begin to think through all this information, start by asking yourself, "Is *sakab* in Genesis 19:32–38 used in the same way it is used in Ruth 3, or is it the exact opposite?" As you look at the similarities, you must factor in the differences. Do you think verse 7 is incidental *or* accidental to the narrative? In other words, what is the narrator's purpose in connecting the wording and plan in Genesis 19:32–38 with Ruth 3? Thoughts?

3. Considering the time it took for verses 6–7 to transpire, can you begin to imagine the risk Ruth was taking? Any thoughts as you process the waiting time? What about Naomi, at home waiting? Have you yet to factor in their faith in all of this or does it apply at all? Do you think they are putting their faith in the character of man?

4. Now, let's look at verse 9. As you compare Naomi's instructions in verses 1–5, do you see Ruth has added something Naomi did not say? Has she gone rogue? Evaluate Ruth's answer when Boaz asks, "Who are you?" Considering the information provided and how the LORD used the word in terms of His covenant in Ezekiel 16:8, how do you interpret her answer? Basically, what is she asking Boaz to do, and upon what and who is she basing her request?

5. Examine Boaz's initial response to Ruth in verses 10–11. Remember, the word "kindness" is translated from the Hebrew word *hesed*. Think about what he says in terms of fear, which is the opposite of faith. What do you see?

a. Do you think Boaz's interpretation of events should drive the way we interpret the entire scenario, including the plan (or scheme, depending on how you interpreted verses 1–5)? And does that change or validate your interpretation thus far? Thoughts?

b. Now compare the wording Boaz used in verse 11 with Proverbs 31:10–31.

**Note**: The exact word *hayil*, translated as "excellence," is used. What do you see? Record your observations about the "woman of excellence" and the correlation of Ruth and Boaz from Proverbs 31:10–31.

The similarities are striking, aren't they? Could these things be said of you?

**Interesting Fact:** "In the Hebrew canonical orders, Ruth is found in the third canonical division (Writings) and put either before Psalms as a kind of biography of the psalmist David, or, more often, placed after Proverbs, making the heroine Ruth an example of 'an excellent wife/worthy woman (Prov. 31:10–31)."[1]

6. Now, let's look at the rest of Boaz's response in verses 12–13. Notice the word *goel* is used six times (close relative, redeem) in these two verses. Remember that this word is attached to Leviticus 25:47–49 and Deuteronomy 25:5–6, and repeated words are used in the Hebrew language for emphasis. Also, keep in mind the three characteristics necessary for the *goel*. Do you sense that a lot is going on in these verses? Record your insights below.

1 Peter H. W. Lau and Gregory Goswell, *Unceasing Kindness: A Biblical Theology of Ruth* (Downers Grove, Ill.: InterVarsity Press, 2016), 23.

7. What is Boaz thinking by giving the closer relative the option to redeem Ruth? Does he not love her? Or does he love someone more? Think about how the LORD instructs His people to love. Look at Deuteronomy 6:5 and Leviticus 19:18 to help answer the question. What do you see?

Now, isn't that true love? When you are willing to forego your happiness for the sake of the LORD and His Word and the sake of the other party involved?

8. As you look at verse 12 and consider the split screen analogy, which includes both the physical and spiritual realm, do you see unbeknownst to Boaz, his words "There is a relative (*goel*) closer than I" are prophetic for both Ruth (and himself)? Thoughts?

   a. Did you catch the play on words with the phrase "as the LORD lives" when used with the term, redeem? For what will it take for the LORD to redeem? Do you see a promise? Does it remind you of the gospel message? Explain your answer as you *look ahead* in the continuing context of the story.

   b. What does his last instruction to "lie down until morning" imply?

*Are you beginning to see the security Naomi prayed for and then acted upon?*

*Scene ten has had a lot to take in, hasn't it?*

## Day Five

### Scene Eleven: Putting the Pieces Together in Ruth 3:14–18

1. Once again, begin today's lesson with prayer.

2. Read the eleventh scene of the narrative, Ruth 3:14–18 and record the people, places, and events in this section below.

I. Who are the people highlighted in this scene?

Next, record the significant place in scene eleven.

II. What place(s) is mentioned in this section? Again, time is relevant.

III. Now, beginning with verse 14, briefly list the events in this scene as they occurred. Consider including the verse numbers.

**Gathering Information:**

Note: In this section, we are told Boaz gave Ruth "six *measures* of barley" to take home (v.15). As you may already know, when you see a word italicized in the Bible, it is not in the original manuscript but has been added for grammatical and translational purposes. Commentators vary on the weight of measurement given, therefore, the amount Boaz gave Ruth is uncertain to us. However, to the Old Testament hearer, it would have been self-evident.

Consider the dilemma among the Hebrew scholars, as Block weighs in, stating,

> Ruth held the garment like a sack while Boaz poured in the grain, six 'measures'of barley. Because the unit of measurement is omitted in the text, it is difficult to calculate the amount of grain Boaz sent home with Ruth. This kind of omission is common in Hebrew, but it is especially frustrating here. If we assume the ephah, the measuring instrument used in 2:17, she would have carried home on her shoulder 180 or 300 pounds, depending on which size ephah is used as the basis of calculation! This is certainly too much for a woman to carry from the field and then up the hill to town.

A more reasonable unit of measurement is the (ʿōmer), which was one-tenth the size of an ephah (Ex. 16:36). By this standard he gave her eighteen or thirty pounds, which is far less than she had gleaned the first day (2:17) but which she would have been able to carry home. A third option is the *seah*, a capacity measure of approximately one third of an ephah, yielding a weight of sixty or one hundred pounds of grain for Ruth to carry. Even if a strong young woman could have carried this amount, it is doubtful whether a cape could hold that much barley. Perhaps the best solution is to assume that the numeral 'six' refers simply to 'six scoops,' either with both hands cupped or with some other handy utensil used at the threshing floor.[1]

Now that we have all the new information, we need to interpret this scene let's start assembling our pieces and place them in the narrative where they belong.

**Putting the Pieces Together**

1. Let's start this section by looking at the phrase, "So she *lay* at his feet until morning." Earlier, we looked at the word *sakab*, which means to lie down with all its implications, but this time, let's look at the phrase considering how it is used in Ruth 3. After all, it is used eight times in this chapter (vv. 4 [3 times], 7 [2 times], 8, 13, and 14), which should alert us to the narrator's purpose by emphasizing the word.

This time, trace who is saying (instructing) *sakab* or doing the action. You should see a pattern: For example,

Who is instructing *sakab* in verse 4? ____________________

Who is obeying *sakab* in verses 7 and 8? __________________

Who is instructing *sakab* in verse 13? ___________________

Who is obeying *sakab* in verse 14? ______________________

2. Now look at Ruth 3:1 and 3:18. Do you see bookends?

**Note:** In literary terms, a bookend is called an *inclusio*, which, when used, focuses the reader's or listener's attention on the chapter's main subject. After discovering the main topic, everything in between serves to help define or describe the main subject.

a. To help you find the main subject, compare Naomi's rhetorical question as she seeks *security* for Ruth with what she said about Boaz in verse 18. What do you see?

b. Now, looking at everything in between, how would you identify the main subject? In other words, who is seen as the object of *security* and *rest*?

c. If you *look ahead* in the biblical narrative, who does this person represent? _________

1 Block, *Judges, Ruth*, Vol. 6, pp. 697–698, accessed April 15, 2023: Logos Bible Software edition.

d. Now, *look back* at Ruth 1:9. Do you see a connection?

3. Now, let's look at Ruth 3:14b. What is Boaz doing here?

Interestingly, what occurred that night is known and recorded in God's eternal Word for all to discover.

4. Now, let's interpret the meaning of the gift of barley in verses 15–17. What are we to make of this gift? Was it to Ruth only?

5. How does Boaz's stated purpose of the gift of barley tie in with Naomi's words in Ruth 1:21?

6. Now look at Isaiah 55:6–11, with particular emphasis on verse 11. Do you see any correlation with Ruth 1:21; 3:17; and Isaiah 55:6–11?

7. What is Naomi's final instruction to Ruth in Ruth 3:18?

**Note:** The word "wait" (*yasab*) means "to sit, dwell, endure, or stay."[1] And the term "turns out" (*napal*) is a verb that means "to fall, to lie, to prostrate oneself."[2]

Can you imagine the wait? Ruth has humbled herself and risked much to obey. But does her hope and future lie only in the man? In other words, Ruth has been asked to wait upon Boaz, but who will ultimately determine the matter? Thoughts?

1 Baker and Carpenter, *The Complete Word Study Dictionary Old Testament*, 479.
2 *Ibid.*, 744.

8. Now, look at what Naomi calls Ruth and count the number of times in this chapter both Naomi and Boaz refer to Ruth in this way. What do you see?

a. The address - ______________________ b. The number of times used ___________

c. What do you think Naomi and Boaz are emphasizing? What are they communicating to Ruth?

9. Are there any additional comments or lingering questions you may have regarding this particular scene?

10. Next, before we leave Ruth 3, compare what you have just studied with Genesis 2:18–25. Any similarities? Record your observations below.

**Note:** Although the Genesis account is Pre-Fall, Ruth 3 has similarities because the providence of God is what is driving the story.

Finally, in summation, as you considered Ruth 3, you had to grapple with questions such as:

Was Naomi a meddling mother-in-law?

Did she take matters into her own hands?

Was she scheming to get her will?

Did she manipulate the situation using seduction?

Was she acting and counseling in her flesh?

Or...

Was she staking all on the LORD, His Word, and upon His providence?

Did we just see an amazing display of faith?

Was she giving counsel by God's Spirit?

In the final summation, only the LORD truly knows her heart's motive, and the narrator doesn't tell us. In fact, the narrator's ambiguity is not accidental. However, a close look at Boaz, as he interprets her actions, is beneficial.

To help us think through these things, consider the following visual of the New Testament Believer.

11. Do you see why the narrator leaves us guessing? As you look at the visual, can you see how both/and are possible explanations for the questions above? Explain your answer.

I realize we just explained the New Testament answer, yet we are dealing with an Old Testament story. The Spirit did not come to live within man until after the finished work of Christ Jesus on the cross (see Ezek. 36:27; Jn. 14:26; 16:7, 13: Acts 2:4). However, the Spirit would come upon individuals to accomplish God's will and Word in the Old Testament. And never forget Who is driving the narrative!

12. In conclusion, you might say the narrator deliberately chose conflicting words to cause the reader to "thresh and winnow" and separate faith from doubt and the flesh from the Spirit.

Therefore, if you had to land somewhere hard, upon which do you think Naomi, Ruth, and Boaz were acting? Do you think they acted upon God's Word by His Spirit or in their flesh? And, if you believe the Spirit and the Word, does that remove the temptation of the flesh or his propensity to make his plans? Explain your answer below. Loaded questions, aren't they?

*Our next lesson will be the climax of all we have been waiting for and then some.*

*Are you ready to see how all this ends?*

Spoiler alert—Providence Prevails!

**Personal Reflections**

Throughout history, theologians, Bible teachers, and commentators have wrestled between two possible and viable interpretations of Ruth 3. In the lesson, I have presented both sides and left it to the student and their residing Built-in Teacher—God's indwelling Spirit, to "instruct, teach, and counsel" (Ps. 32:8).

With your permission, I would like to share what I believe He has shown me using the Scriptures to validate the position I have taken (at least at this point in my spiritual walk).

First, I do not take the position of the scheming mother-in-law.

I see Naomi as one who has been given the "bitter" experience of trauma, loss, and great grief (Ruth 1:3, 5). And yet, as with every bitter experience, two roads can be taken: one will either become bitter, or one will emerge from the trauma and loss "better," in terms of a genuine faith refined in the fire of affliction. That stated, the determining factor in a bitter situation becomes where one turns. With the repetition of the word "return" (used 12 times in Ruth 1:6–22), I see a woman who is "turning" (looking) to God for her salvation (Isa. 45:22) in her very "bitter" situation.

By "returning" to the LORD and His people, she is looking to His character, namely, *hesed* (lovingkindness), and His Word, specifically the promise concerning the levirate marriage in Deuteronomy 25:5–10. In other words, Naomi's faith was being tested, while Ruth's faith was being established. Will they take God at His Word? Will they believe in who He is, as He says He is in His Word? Will they come to experientially know the God who proclaimed Himself as "The LORD, the LORD God, compassionate and gracious, slow to anger, and abounding in lovingkindness (*hesed*) and truth" (Ex. 34:6)?

You see, faith isn't genuine saving faith until it is tested. And faith requires action—an absolute surrender to God's will in obedience to His Word. I believe Ruth 3 is a "radical" all-or-nothing surrender of the will of Naomi and Ruth in obedience to God's character and Word. This type of faith is willing to humble oneself and risk reputation and comfort by flinging all on Him. It's the kind of response to God's Word that willingly risks being misrepresented and misunderstood, one when actions may be misinterpreted. It's what I call a free-fall on who He says He is and what He promises, and it's deeply personal. After all, the total surrender of one's will and obedience to God's Word is "better than sacrifice" (1 Sam. 15:22). Therefore, I believe Naomi's counsel and Ruth's actions are just that—a total surrender of will in obedience that is willing to risk all on who He says He is and what He says He will do.

So, what about the specific words and phrases used in the narrative lend to the controversy?

Allow me to address each beginning with the instruction to "wash, anoint yourself, and put on your cloak," which, when viewed according to the flesh, some could interpret as her way of seducing Boaz. However, we saw the exact words used in 2 Samuel 12:20 about David after the death of his son with Bathsheba. As we looked at 2 Samuel 12, we saw David bowing in worship in surrender to God's will, which included death. Isn't that what occurs when faith is tested? Does it not involve the death of one's will to God's?

Furthermore, I do not feel the instruction to "uncover his feet" is a reference to his genitalia, as such an interpretation does not fit the context given throughout the narrative (Ruth 3:4, 7) because the adjoining phrase is for her to "lie down." So, is one to assume Naomi instructs Ruth to uncover and lie down on his genitalia? Similarly, as Ruth carries out her instructions in verse 7, she "uncovered his feet and lay down." Moreover, in the next verse, Boaz is startled as he "bent forward" to discover a "woman was lying at his feet" (Ruth 3:8). Again, are we to assume she positioned herself on his genitalia?

Even more telling is Boaz's response, which can help us understand her actions and intentions for he sees them as kindness (v. 10) and her as a "woman of excellence" (v. 11). Would he say that about a woman who was seducing him by exposing his genitalia? And again, in verse 14, when Boaz instructs Ruth to "lie down until morning" (v. 13), and Scripture records, "So she lay at his feet until morning" (v. 14), I do not think she positioned herself any other place than his literal feet. What do you think?

In other words, to take one phrase and make it seductive, one has to use that interpretation throughout the narrative, correct?

In summary, I believe Naomi's instruction and Ruth's obedience are acts of faith in who God is—for lovingkindness is a covenant term used with God as the source that Naomi and Ruth can see and trust in Boaz. I believe their use of the term, *goel*, or kinsman-redeemer, directly indicates that they are taking God at His Word—trusting everything: their security and future, their reputation, and their hope in who God is and what God said. Boaz is merely the human instrument God chose to display His lovingkindness and care.

I also believe the place of the threshing floor lends to this interpretation, for Ruth must "go down" (v.6) to the threshing floor to obey Naomi's instructions. Symbolically, the threshing floor represented a place of humility, separation (the beating and removal of chaff), and revelation (the true wheat). And faith that is tested will require humility and separation, yet it will result in a greater revelation of who God is and a deeper trust in what He says, and both will result in true worship. It will also reveal those with genuine saving faith.

In conclusion, the lesson closed with the difference between the flesh and the Spirit. To help distinguish between the two, in the lesson, we examined the reference in Genesis 19 with Lot's daughters (Ruth's ancestral beginning) to compare the events. With the correlation of events, the student of the Bible is invited to examine both texts closely to compare and ascertain the correct interpretation. This is just good biblical hermeneutics (the interpretation of Scripture).

Upon close examination, although eerily close encounters, the motivations of Lot's daughters become clear and are quite different than those of Naomi and Ruth. For Lot's daughters, assuming it is their job to "preserve our family through our father" (Gen. 19:32), make him drunk so that Lot neither knew when his daughters "lay down or arose" (Gen. 19:33, 35). In fact, they are taking matters into their own hands based on their knowledge of their dire circumstances (see Gen. 19:31).

In contrast, Naomi and Ruth place their hope and confidence in God and His Word. They are entreating the LORD to "preserve" the family and preserve what He will do, for He will send His own Son through the seed of the union of Boaz and Ruth (Mt. 1:5). But that is a story for another lesson, and in our final lesson, we will witness how the entire narrative points to Christ!

In the meantime, we leave Naomi and Ruth in chapter 3, waiting on the LORD.

# Lesson 5

## The Lord's Providence Prevails

RUTH 4:1–22

We left off last week with what many may call a cliffhanger. Ruth executed what appears to be Naomi's plan. But was Naomi conspiring and cooking up a risky scheme, as some have interpreted, or was she taking a leap of faith and staking all on the Lord and His Word?

Regardless of Naomi's intent, Ruth followed her mother-in-law's counsel, and by risking everything, she proposed marriage to Boaz, and he accepted. But as you will recall, there was a glitch in the plan. It wasn't quite that easy. For there was another kinsman, a closer relative than Boaz, and he had to be factored in, right? Well, only if you are a righteous man of integrity. Otherwise, who would have to know? Boaz and Ruth could have acted in the flesh that night in the field and taken matters into their own hands. But God's providence has been driving things from the story's very first sentence and will continue to do so.

And we simply do not know whether Boaz and Ruth faced sexual temptation in this field, for those details were left out of the story. What we do know, they both chose to act in keeping with the character and the Word of God, and we also know they managed to do this only by the grace of God. And the personal decisions they make in a secret place are about to become decidedly established and legally confirmed in a very public place. Isn't it interesting that faith was privately tested on the threshing floor and in the darkness before it was publicly known at the gate? Isn't that true of all faith?

Let's see how Boaz proceeds in what has now become a legal matter. Naomi and Ruth's redemption depends on it. In fact, first and foremost, redemption in any case is a legal matter before a just, righteous, and holy God.

Are you ready to bring this story to its conclusion? Let's get started.

### Day One

### Scene 12: Putting the Pieces Together in Ruth 4:1–6

1. Begin today's lesson with prayer.
2. Read the twelfth scene of the narrative, Ruth 4:1–6 and record the people, places, and events in this section in the space provided on the next page.

I. Who are the people in these verses? List them in the order they occur in the story. (Consider including the verse numbers.)

Next, record the significant place in scene twelve.

II. What place(s) is mentioned in this section? Time is also a factor here.

III. Now, beginning with verse 1, briefly list the events in this scene as they occurred. Consider including the verse numbers.

**Gathering Information:**

Note: The term "gate" of the city designated the city's meeting place and entrance. Figuratively, it represented the place of prominence and leadership. It was the place where legal and business matters were heard, negotiated, and confirmed. It was a place that represented fact gathering, wisdom, and counsel.

Similarly, the "elders" represented the older, wiser, and more mature men of the city. The Hebrew term translated "elders" here also carries the idea of "dignity, rank, and privilege."[1] These men were the leaders of the city, decision makers who could serve as witnesses in biblical and legal matters.

**Putting the Pieces Together**

1. What do you notice immediately in terms of timing (v. 1) as to the previous night's event?

2. Notice the words, "behold, the close relative (*gō'ēl*) . . . was passing by." What does the narrator want you to be sure to behold? Is this another coincidence, or a chance encounter? Whom and what do you see?

Did you notice the repetitive words "sat down" and the invitation to "sit down" in verses 1–2? You may not know that the exact Hebrew word, translated as "wait," is used in Naomi's instruction to Ruth in 3:18. It will be used again in 4:4.

1 Baker and Carpenter, *The Complete Word Study Dictionary Old Testament*, 300.

3. What is the narrator emphasizing? To help understand the meaning of yā·šāḇ (wait), you must consider that its definition is not limited to one's physical location but can also represent one's position or stance in the matter. In essence, everyone takes their position or role in the case.

a. Look at each party to determine their position in the particular matter. In the space provided, record each person's position or role below.

Ruth and Naomi (3:18)

Boaz (4:4) Notice his position

The unnamed man (4:1, 3) Notice what he is called.

The word "friend" in verse 1 is not an accurate translation. In fact, the Hebrew is *pelōnī ʾalmōnī*, "two rhyming nouns of similar but not identical formation."[1] It's a play on words, better translated as "Mr. So-and-so."[2]

1) What is his initial position on the matter (v. 4)? ________________________

2) What is his final position with all the facts (v. 6)? ________________________

The ten elders (4:11) Notice what they are called. ______________________________

Something significant to consider as we view the scene at the gate of decision—everyone is seated and taking their position in the matter. While on the other screen, the One who has called the meeting is sitting on His throne, overseeing the entire case.

Meanwhile, did you see who is assembling the ten elders and the *gōʾēl* to sit? Does that say something about Boaz's position and reputation among the leaders in the city?

4. Next, let's determine the matter at hand. To do so, read verses 4–6. Do you see a repeated word and its synonym? If so, what is it, and how many times is it used in these three verses?

You are probably understanding that this scenario has become a matter of redemption In fact, it is now a legal transaction, which is why it is being carried out in public with witnesses.

5. Before we go further in the lesson, it would be helpful to read Numbers 27:8–11 where the Lord established a set order in reference to one's inheritance. Record the order below.

1 Edward F. Campbell, J., *Ruth: A New Translation with Introduction, Notes, and Commentary*, Vol. 7, (New Haven, CT.; Yale University, 2008), 141, accessed April 22, 2023: Logos Bible Software edition.

2 *Ibid.*

6. Next, consider how Boaz addresses the matter of redemption before the closest relative (*goel*) and the ten elders (witnesses) he asks to sit with in verses 3–6. Does he immediately ask for Ruth's hand? Is that the central issue on his mind? Carefully notice with whom he begins his concern. As you think through these things, consider that the Hebrew word translated "come back" is the same word translated "return" (repent) in Chapter 1, where we saw it used twelve times. In addition, the words "raise up" literally means "to revive."[1]Using this terminology, what is Boaz saying about Naomi, and why does that matter?

Record your insights into the order, words, and way Boaz speaks.

According to Mosaic Law, the land was never to leave the family because the Lord had initially apportioned it to each tribe. Ultimately the land belonged to the Lord (Lev. 25:23). In fact, the Lord established the year of Jubilee every fifty years to ensure that if sold out of poverty, land could return to the original family for their inheritance (see Leviticus 25 to learn more about the year of Jubilee).

Therefore, Naomi is not transferring the ownership of the land but instead authorizing the *gōʾēl* the legal right to use the land until the year of Jubilee. Boaz, in effect, is conducting the legalities on her behalf.[2]

7. With these things noted, what does Boaz state as his primary concern? In other words, what is the purpose of deciding the matter of redemption in verse 5?

Next, we see two people at the crossroads of decision in the matter of redemption. Except this time, it's two men.

1 Baker and Carpenter, *The Complete Word Study Dictionary Old Testament*, 987.

2 Block, *Judges, Ruth*, Vol. 6, 710, accessed April 25, 2023: Logos Bible Software edition.

8. What are the terms of redemption? In other words, is it going to be free and personally beneficial? Do you see that each are being asked their position (or where they "sit") on who the Lord truly is and what He says in His Word? What do you see in each man's response?

As you think through each man's decision, you will encounter the word "jeopardize" (*sahat*), which means "to spoil, corrupt, pervert" in verse 6.[1]

Do you recall the three conditions necessary to qualify as kinsman redeemer (*gō'ēl*) from our last lesson?

- He had to be a family member
- He had to have the power and ability (i.e., financially) to redeem
- He had to be willing

With the information given, evaluate each man's response? Do you see either man displaying *hesed*?

Boaz –

The unnamed *gō'ēl* –

9. As you reflect on each man's position, look at Psalm 1, where the same Hebrew word for "sits" is used. Notice that where a man sits and with whom he sits is instructive. What do you see? Record your insights.

10. How do you evaluate both men in terms of what Jesus said in Mark 8:34?

In this section, I found the words of pastor and author Alistair Begg most helpful as he simplified the transaction presented by Boaz. Basically, the closest relative (*gō'ēl*), "Mr. So and So," was given two parts to the legal transaction. First, Boaz presented the nearest heir with an amazing opportunity to purchase more property. But secondly, along with this profitable purchase, there was also a duty, for with the property came a widow and the obligation

1 Baker and Carpenter, *The Complete Word Study Dictionary Old Testament*, 1124.

of marriage. And with marriage, there came the danger of a new heir, which would "jeopardize" the inheritance for his children. In other words, the *gō'ēl* had the right to purchase the property, but with that opportunity, there was a chance that his estate would legally go to the widow's child resulting in nothing for the children of the *gō'ēl*, the one who purchased the property.[1]

In essence, the transaction required a selfless and costly obedience with no guarantee of benefit to the *gō'ēl*. Only those who value obedience and trust the Lord and His Word would take the risk.

11. Now, do you see the brilliant way in which the narrator frames the story? Compare the crossroads scenario from Ruth 1 with the crossroads encounter in Ruth 4. [You will recall when Orpah and Ruth stood at a crossroads with Naomi, and each made a critical life decision (Ruth 1:14), so too, Mr. So-and-So and Boaz are making a crossroads decision. Each will make their choice, which will change the course of their lives forever.] Record your insights below.

Keep this in mind as the decision is sealed, witnessed, and evaluated in the next scene.

## Days Two and Three

## Scene 13: Putting the Pieces Together in Ruth 4:7–12

1. Begin today's lesson with prayer.

2. Read the thirteenth scene of the narrative, Ruth 4:7–12 and record the people, places, and events in this section below.

I. Who are the people in these verses? List them in the order they occur in the story. (Consider including the verse numbers.)

1 Alistair Begg, "So Boaz Took Ruth," accessed November 4, 2023: [on-line] available at https://www.truthforlife.org/resources/sermon/so-boaz-took-ruth/

Places

II. Next, record the significant place(s) in this scene

Events

III. Now, beginning with verse 7, briefly list the events in this scene as they occurred. Consider including the verse numbers.

**Gathering Information:**
First, in verse seven, the narrator gives the reader some additional information to which they may not be privy. He reminds the reader of a custom that took place in the time of the judges when the story of Ruth takes place.

**Note:** Although the date and authorship of Ruth are unnamed, the ancient teachings of the Talmud attributes Samuel as the author of Ruth (and Judges).[1]

So, what was the ancient way of signing a legal agreement in the days of the book of Ruth? According to the narrator, a legal matter was settled publicly among trusted elders of the city who served as witnesses (vv. 1–6), according to Deuteronomy 25:7–10 when one party removed his sandal and gave it to the other party as a matter of attestation (confirmation, corroboration) in Israel before all to see (verse 7).

**Putting the Pieces Together**
1. Read Ruth 4:7 and then read Deuteronomy 25:7–10 with emphasis on verses 9–10. What seems to be missing from the encounter in Ruth, and why might this be so? Any thoughts?

2. Now, record your insights from Ruth 4:8–10 as the redemption transaction occurs. What do you see? Pay close attention to Boaz's response. In other words, to whom and what was Boaz assuming responsibility (vv. 9–10)? Was it the personal acquisition of both the land and a wife? Or was there a deeper level of involvement that required hesed, integrity, and honor toward the Lord and His Word? Record your insights.

3. With that answered, what did the unnamed *gōʾēl's* choice prove about himself, and ultimately what did that cost him in the end?

1 Block, *Judges, Ruth*, Vol. 6, 590, accessed April 22, 2023: Logos Bible Software edition.

A costly decision for the unnamed *gōʾēl'*, wouldn't you say? In fact, unlike Orpah, he remains unnamed, but like Orpah, his name, family, and inheritance are never mentioned again.

4. Now, in terms of the split-screen, let's look at redemption by looking closely at verse 10 again. Why does Boaz keep using words like "death" and "inheritance"? And what spiritual connotation does that imply? Romans 6:23 may be helpful. Knowing that the "wages of sin" result in death, think in terms of it not just being only a physical matter but also spiritual, in terms of a legal case between humanity and a holy and righteous God.

Furthermore, from verse 10, the words "raise up" which, as you saw in verse 5, means "to revive." Why do you think Boaz was so concerned with the "dead" and their "inheritance"? Do you see any spiritual connection? It may help to review and include 1 Peter 1:3–5 in your answer. Record your insights.

Do you see on the split-screen that there is far more at stake than Boaz gaining the personal possession of land and a wife? He is not just being "nice," but rather, he is being obedient and selfless, honoring God and giving Him glory as God.

5. Now let's bring in the witnesses from verses 11–12. What purpose do they serve in these verses? What do you see them doing in general?

6. Let's examine their prayer a little closer now. Notice they pray for "the woman who is coming into your home" first. Then they compare her with Rachel and Leah in the same verse, connecting Rachel and Leah with "wealth" and being "famous." As you think about each woman's part in Israel's history, what are they asking the Lord on behalf of Ruth?

**Note:** To help answer this question, allow me to define a few Hebrew words:

"Built"—(*banah*) is used figuratively in Genesis 2:22 when Eve is "built" from Adam's rib, not created separately. It is used in Deuteronomy 25:9, the Levirate passage, to build a family. In Psalm 89:2, it is used by the Lord, who said, "lovingkindness (*hesed*) will be built up forever."[1]

"Wealth"—(*hayil*) is better translated as "strength and influence." It is used to describe virtuous character.[2] You may recognize this word as it was used to describe Boaz in 2:1, and later Boaz used it to describe Ruth in 3:11.

"Famous"—(*sem*) to obtain a reputation, name, or standing. It is used in Deuteronomy 25:7, the Levirate passage,

1 Baker and Carpenter, *The Complete Word Study Dictionary Old Testament*, 145.
2 *Ibid.*, 334.

to continue the name of a man, a family line, which gave him an ongoing life in his sons.[1]

7. Next, they pray over Boaz's house. To whom do they compare it, and what is the significance of the request? See Genesis 38 if you are unfamiliar with the account of Perez, whose name means, "breach, to tear, or separation."[2] Record any similarities and the significance of Boaz and his house.

Did you see their prayer included the promise of a progeny (offspring)? Is that another "P" we can add to Yahweh in terms of Place, Provision, and Protection?

8. Before we close this section, let's return to our first observation in Ruth 4, and look at where everyone involved in redemption sat or positioned themselves. But this time, record where each positioned or set themselves regarding the LORD and His Word. What do you see?

    a. Ruth (and Naomi) see 2:12 and 3:9—____________________________________

    b. Boaz – ____________________________________________________________

    c. The unnamed *gō'ēl'*—__________________________________________________

    d. The elders and witnesses—_______________________________________________

Again, do you see one's place or position (to sit) regarding the eternal Lord and His Word is what determines one's eternal provision and protection?

9. That's enough to consider for the time being. We will pick back up in scene fourteen as we cover Ruth 4:13–17 tomorrow. For now, meditate on what you have seen so far. If there are any additional insights or questions you have, feel free to record them in space provided on the next page.

1 *Ibid.*, 1157.
2 *Ibid.*, 922.

## Day Four

### Scene 14: Putting the Pieces Together in Ruth 4:13–17

1. Begin today's lesson with prayer.
2. Read the thirteenth scene of the narrative, Ruth 4:13–17 and record the people, places, and events in this section below.

I. Who are the people in these verses? List them in the order they occur in the story. (Consider including the verse numbers.)

Next, record the significant place(s) in this scene.

II. What place(s) is mentioned in this section?

III. Now, beginning with verse 13, briefly list the events in this scene as they occur. Consider including the verse numbers.

**Gathering Information:**
Let's begin by defining the words "restorer" and "sustainer."

First, the word "restorer" in verse 15 is a familiar term, and it comes from the Hebrew word *sub*, which, as you will recall from chapter one, is used twelve times, and means "to bring back, to return."[1] The literal Hebrew translation of the phrase "restorer of life" is "one who causes life to return."[2] Additionally, the Hebrew word translated "sustainer" in verse 15 literally means "to hold, feed, supply."[3]

**Putting the Pieces Together**

1. Notice all that takes place in verse 13 for it is jam-packed. Although we are not specifically told, at least nine months is covered in only one verse. What do you see?

As you think about just how far Ruth has come since we first were introduced to her in Ruth 1:4, Ruth 4:13 is like her coronation, and she represents a beautiful picture today. Recording the progression, Dr. Block explains, stating, "In 'becoming his wife,' Ruth's social progression is completed. She had graduated from the status of *nokriyyâ*, 'foreigner' (2:10), to *šipḥâ*, 'lowest servant' (2:13), to *'āmâ*, 'maidservant' (3:9), and now to *'iššâ*, 'wife.' "[4]

With that in mind, think about how far we "Ruths" have come because of our Redeemer. From foreigners and slaves to sin, to becoming slaves to righteousness, to being the Bride of Christ. Do you see justification, sanctification, and glorification?

Oh, the *hesed* (lovingkindness), hen (grace), and *ahavah* (love) of our Lord! Blessed Redeemer! Did you also notice who was directly involved in her ability to conceive?

2. As you think about the fact that the LORD had closed Ruth's womb in Moab, what do you see regarding God and His providence and timing? Do you think He knows what He is doing and has a far bigger plan than anyone in the story could have previously known? Think through how His timing affected everyone in the narrative? What are some of your thoughts?

3. Next, the women in the city re-enter the scene. What are they doing in verses 14–15? Notice what they say in terms of the LORD, the child, Ruth, and Naomi? Record your insights below.

1 Baker and Carpenter, The Complete Word Study Dictionary Old Testament, 1108.

2 Edward F. Campbell, J., *Ruth: A New Translation with Introduction, Notes, and Commentary,* Vol. 7 (New Haven, CT.; Yale University, 2008), 164, accessed April 22, 2023: Logos Bible Software edition.

3 Baker and Carpenter, The Complete Word Study Dictionary Old Testament, 499.

4 Block, *Judges, Ruth,* Vol. 6, 725, accessed April 25, 2023: Logos Bible Software edition.

Initially, the first sentence (v. 14) of their blessing appears as if they are referring to Boaz, but as you look carefully at verse 15, you soon realize they are referring to the child, Obed. So, what are we to make of this?

Old Testament scholars Peter Lau and Gregory Goswell help here by explaining the matter more fully, stating,

> It is surprising that Obed is identified as a kinsman-redeemer, since elsewhere the Old Testament a redeemer is always an adult. How does Obed function in this way? When Obed grows up, he will protect and provide for Naomi in her old age (4:15), a role usually given to biological sons. Even as a child he 'redeems' Naomi from bitterness and emptiness (1:20-21), for now 'a son' has been born to her (4:17). Although they can never be fully replaced, the sons (yeladim: 1:5) she lost have been replaced by this son (yeled; 4:17). Of course, Obed is not literally Naomi's son; indeed, the baby is not even related to her by blood since his parents are Naomi's daughter-in-law and a relative of her deceased husband's. However, through the working of the levirate law, the son is in Elimelech's line and so is legally hers. Thus, consistent with the meaning of his name, 'servant', Obed serves Naomi both in his birth and when he is fully grown.[1]

Do you see why Boaz made the situation a legal matter? Can you see that by following the law (Deuteronomy 25:5–10), the LORD is redeeming Naomi while preserving the names of the dead so that both Elimelech and Mahlon will not be blotted out from Israel (Deut. 25:6)? Can you also see that the redemption is through the selflessness of Boaz and the birth of Obed?

Now, look again at verse 15. Did you see the word "love"?

Is it surprising that this is the first and only time it is used in the entire narrative? Directly linked with lovingkindness (*hesed*) and grace (*hen*), the verb *ahab* (love) is used here.

Typically, when the word "love" is used today, it is associated with emotions and only feeling-based, and therefore, it can ebb and flow as the situation/person warrants. That is not the kind of love the Word is explaining. In fact, the love mentioned in the verses above and Ruth 4:15 finds its basis in the Source of love—the Lord GOD.

However, in Hebrew, love is never just a feeling, but is always interconnected with action, which, in turn, involves the will. In fact, love is "expressed in acts of *ḥesed*, placing the welfare of the other ahead of oneself."[2] To better understand the Hebrew use of love, look at the following cross-references where the noun ahavah is used.

4. Let's look at Scripture for the definition and record your observations regarding "love."

    a. Deuteronomy 6:5 ____________________________________________

    ______________________________________________________________

    b. Leviticus 19:18 ____________________________________________

    ______________________________________________________________

    c. Leviticus 19:34 ____________________________________________

    ______________________________________________________________

5. Now, as you look at these references, do you see an order? And although the word love is not mentioned, can you see how Boaz ultimately displayed his love as he obeyed the law? Record your thoughts.

---

1 Peter H. W. Lau and Gregory Goswell, *Unceasing Kindness: A Biblical Theology of Ruth*, (Downers Grove, IL: InterVarsity Press, 2016), 118.

2 Block, *Judges, Ruth*, Vol. 6, 729, accessed April 24, 2023: Logos Bible Software edition.

In short, Boaz demonstrated his love for the Lord, Naomi, and Ruth (and in that order) by obeying God's Word. Isn't that the order in which the Bible places how our love is to be displayed?

6. Isn't it ironic that the word love is stated only once in the Book of Ruth, and that it is connected to and displayed in a Moabite woman? Can you trace the love Ruth has demonstrated from the beginning? And finally, any thoughts to the comparison of Ruth's love being better than seven sons (v. 15)?

Consider the following additional information by Dr. Block as he comments on the comparison, stating,

> The reference to 'seven sons' is conventional, reflecting the ancient Israelite view that the ideal family consisted of seven sons. This is an amazing affirmation of the character of Ruth. All Bethlehem knew she was a noble woman (3:11), but these women place her value above seven sons; what extraordinary compensation for the two sons Naomi had lost![1]

Have you ever wondered how Ruth must have felt when Naomi told the women in the city she had come back "empty" when Ruth was standing next to her? Obviously, that was Naomi's perspective. However, from the Lord's perspective, she had everything she needed and was actually quite full but didn't know it yet.

7. Now, consider how this encounter with the women in the city contrasts and compares with their meeting in Ruth 1:19–21. Record your insights.

8. Compare Naomi's statement, "I went out full, but the LORD has brought me back empty" (1:21), with Ruth 4:16–17. Had the LORD emptied her, the obvious answer is "Yes!," but for what purpose? For the LORD does nothing in vain. If He afflicts, it is always for the purpose of filling. He is actually saving, for that is what His name LORD means. Compare what He had emptied with how He filled the emptiness. What do you see?

**Note:** The Hebrew word translated "nurse" in 4:16 is more akin to a "guardian rather than a wet nurse."[2]

9. As to taking a literal translation of the women naming Obed, many commentators do not believe they actually named the baby boy as much as they highlighted the meaning of his name, which means to serve. As you look at verses 16–17, how would his life serve immediately and in the future?

---

1 Block, *Judges, Ruth*, Vol. 6, 729, accessed April 22, 2023: Logos Bible Software edition.

2 Edward F. Campbell, J., *Ruth: A New Translation with Introduction, Notes, and Commentary*, Vol. 7, (New Haven, CT.; Yale University, 2008), 165, accessed April 22, 2023: Logos Bible Software edition.

10. Now before we bring this section to a close, compare Naomi's prayer in 1:8–9 with what has transpired in chapters two through four? What do you see?

## Day Five

### Scene 15: Putting the Pieces Together in Ruth 4:18–22

1. Begin today's lesson with prayer.
2. Read the final scene of the narrative, Ruth 4:18-22 and record the people in this section below.

I. Who are the people in these verses? List them in the order they occur in the story.

Can you see that what began with no king in Israel, famine, barrenness, and death now ends in one of Israel's greatest kings coming, the provision of food, a child, and life?

II. And finally, look at the culmination of Obed's lineage in Matthew 1:1–16 with emphasis on verses 5–6 and 16. What and who do you see?

Do you clearly see how God's providence began with "Now it came about..." and ended this story, "Now these are the generations of Perez..."?

*Talk about a CLIMAX!*

*Can this story get any better than Christ?*

Our final lesson will focus entirely on Christ and how He is the One to whom the story points. But for now, in closing, let's take some time to allow God's Spirit to use the book of Ruth to apply some of these truths to our hearts. In this section, prayerfully ask yourself each of these questions. And note, there may be more the Spirit will bring to mind as you examine His Word.

**What About You?**

1. Have you turned from the "house of bread" (from the Lord and His people) to seek comfort, pleasure, or answers from the world? Is the Lord calling you back to Himself? Will you turn?

Psalm 34:6 records, "This poor man (woman) cried, and the LORD heard and saved them out of all their troubles." Therefore, if you can identify with Elimelech, the answer is to cry out! He will hear and He will save!

OR...

2. Do you identify most with Naomi, whose life is encompassed by death? Have you turned to the LORD in your sorrow?

Remember, death can take many forms: whether physical death has occurred in the loss of a spouse, a child, a family member, or a close friend, the end of a marriage, a dream, hope, a deep desire, the loss of a job, a promotion, a friendship, a ministry, or even, your reputation? Basically, any unmet expectation can fall into this category.

Believe it or not, the most important question is not what has happened, but to whom and where have you turned?

I read an excellent article by Carolyn Mahaney entitled "Hope for Your Unhappy Life."[1] In the article, Carolyn shared how the Lord used the book of Ecclesiastes to "graciously free me from my despair and helped me find peace and joy" in the middle of the storm she and her family were facing. She highlighted one verse, in particular, that stood out to her, which states, "It is an unhappy business that God has given to the children of man to be busy with" (Eccl. 1:13). She goes on to add the part that stood out most were the words, "that God has given." And for all of us who believe in the providence of God, we would all agree, for God uses both the good and the evil to conform us to the image of His dear Son (Rom. 8:29).

In the article, she used two words that were very timely for my heart to consider, "misplaced hope." You see, the things He puts to death in our life can devastate our hearts but are necessary, because if we are honest with ourselves, we find that unknowingly and sometimes willfully, in them, we have somehow misplaced our hope.

As you think about Naomi's statement, "I went out full, but the LORD has brought me back empty," how many of us can say the same thing, especially when death tragically and sometimes suddenly interrupts our life?

And what seems even worse and even more challenging to reconcile in our minds is that God has been the giver of the tragedy. How are we to turn to the One who could have stopped it from happening? But turn we must! Although we do not understand His ways or thoughts, deep down, we know He is the LORD GOD. And our only hope is to "Look to Him," for He alone can save (Isa. 45:22).

At these times, we cry, "Cause me to look to You, O LORD. Cause me to turn because apart from You, I cannot."

---

1 Carolyn Mahaney, "Hope for Your Unhappy Life," [on-line]; accessed April 13, 2023; available at https://www.desiringgod.org/articles/hope-for-your-unhappy-life; Internet.

Will He watch over His Word to perform it in your heart (Jer. 1:12)? Ask Him. Turn to Him. Watch Him do for you what you are unable to do for yourself.

Do you find yourself here? Is the Lord saving you from some "misplaced hope" you didn't even know existed? Are you having trouble trusting the One who says, "He is good, and He does good" (Ps. 119:68: emphasis added)? Ask Him to cause you to turn to Him. And as you do, watch as He heals your broken heart and gives you "exceedingly abundantly beyond all that we ask or think" (Eph. 3:20).

And remember, as with Naomi, the answer may be down the road, and in fact, it may not be revealed until we step into eternity. Rest assured, in the end, we will see that it brought glory to our God and was ultimately for our good.

How could Ruth have ever seen that the death that completely encompassed her heart in the first chapter would ultimately culminate in the Giver of Life? To the praise of His glory and for her (and our) good.

OR...

3. Have you been praying Ruth 1:8–9 for those you know and love? Are you turning to the Lord asking Him to "deal kindly" and "grant rest" to those who do not know Him?

OR...

4. Have you found yourself, like Ruth and Orpah, at the crossroads of decision while doing the study? Has His Spirit shown you through the book of Ruth that you have not turned from your idols to serve the living God?

Again, the answer to this dilemma is to cry out! He will hear and He will save you!

OR...

5. Has Providence brought you to His field of grace? Are you gleaning from His lovingkindness (*hesed*) and favor (*hen*)? Are you joyfully and gratefully giving Him the praise He is due? Are you sharing His lovingkindness and grace with others?

OR...

6. Has Providence placed you in a difficult circumstance or with challenging people? Maybe you are in an impossible situation from your standpoint. Are you finding His wings to be the shelter you need for place, provision, and protection? To whom or what have you been running for refuge and shelter?

OR...

7. With whom do you sit (position yourself regularly), and where do you find rest? Do you find yourself in a time of waiting on the Lord to save you or someone you love? Are you waiting with a restful heart or wringing your hands in anxiety?

Again, the answer will be to whom and where you run. Your prayer, "Lord, I find my heart filled with anxious thoughts. Cause me to trust what Your Word declares in Psalm 94:19, 'When anxious thoughts multiply within me, Your Word delights my soul.' " Cry out, "Lord, send Your Word to heal me" (see Ps. 107:20).

OR...

8. Has he sent His Word, and you are at the crossroads of a decision whether to obey or not? Has He, through His Spirit and Word, directed your path down a road that will require an incredible leap of faith? A way you

would never have chosen for yourself? Maybe the path is leading you down in humiliation. Perhaps no one will understand and, in fact, think you are crazy or even taking things a bit too far. Your reputation may get tarnished in the eyes of others. Are you willing? If not, ask Him to cause you to obey His Word, no matter how risky. Let no one and nothing stand in the way of you and your Savior!

OR...

9. Is the issue of obedience not what it is costing you but those you love? Although the cost to self may be difficult, typically, the greater rub for me is when it involves those I love most. That's when it seems unbearable, right?

Are you willing to trust those you love with Him?

OR...

10. Do you sense the LORD may be emptying you? Could it be for the purpose of filling you with more of Himself? Is there anything or anyone greater? Could following Him result in something far greater than you could have ever imagined possible? Do you believe "Eye has not seen, and ear has not heard and have not entered the heart of man, all that God has prepared for those who love Him" (1 Cor. 2:9)?

And the list could go on. Feel free to allow His Spirit to reveal and press another situation addressed in the book of Ruth to your heart.

OR...

Could it be a time to wash your face with the water of the Word (Eph. 5:26), remove your mourning clothes and return to the Lord in worship? Maybe it's time to ask the Lord to help you exchange your ashes for garland, mourning for the oil of gladness, and the spirit of fainting for the mantle of praise (Isa. 61:2–3). He is after "oaks of righteousness, the planting of the LORD that He may be glorified" (Isa. 61:3b).

*Have you seen a common thread in all these scenarios?*

*Are you becoming aware that God's providence has placed you in this study for such a time as this?*

*Will you come to the Savior today?*

*He is waiting to save!*

# Notes

# Lesson 6

## The Lord's Providence Unveiled: Our Kinsman-Redeemer

Over the past several lessons, we have been putting the pieces together of a beautiful Old Testament story of everyday people in real-life situations. We have been engaged in the life of one ordinary Jewish family during some very dark and challenging times in Israel's history. We have seen choices made at every turn—some poor, leading to death, and other decisions life-giving. These things have been occurring on the right side of the split-screen analogy we have been using to help us understand the whole picture (or, at least, that side of the image).

But we have discovered, even from the story's first words, that another Divine story was also being unveiled. We have learned that this story drives Ruth's story and every story that will ever be told. In other words, it's not only previous; it is preeminent. And hopefully, before the end of this lesson, you will discover that it is also precious!

Therefore, in this lesson we will narrow our focus on a very different screen, one on which God's eternal counsel is sovereignly and providentially working. Unlike Ruth and the people in her story, we have a fuller picture since we have the whole counsel of God's revealed will—His Word to help us fill in some gaps. So, what has God been doing? Who is the main character in the Book of Ruth? Is it Naomi, Ruth, or Boaz, or has the main character remained hidden? Is the primary purpose of Ruth's story to be just another good story in Scripture, or is there a divine purpose? And does it involve just the stories already told, or is it for us here, now, and even into the future? In other words, does the left side of the screen still affect the story of our life that is taking place on the right side of the screen now?

Could it be that the left side of the screen never changes, because neither God nor His eternal counsel change? We also know His will cannot be thwarted (Job. 42:2). However, the right side of the screen has been changing throughout the course of history, adding new names and circumstances as time goes by? And now, instead of Ruth's story, we could put our name in the box, knowing that God's plan continues to unfold. These are the questions we will address in this lesson, so let's get started.

You will notice this lesson will not be divided into days. The arrangement has been purposeful to allow one continual flow of thought because you will need time to process and make connections, especially in the latter part of the lesson. Are you ready to begin?

You will recall in Lesson One, we established that our sovereign God, in the eternal counsel of God of His will, was, is, and will be providentially at work.

**In other words:** God the Father has the Plan (His Will)

*Through* His beloved Son,

*By* the power of His Spirit (who uses His Word)

We also recognized that He has chosen to progressively reveal Himself in Scripture by His names (who He is) and His works (what He is doing). We began the study by establishing two specific names of God: Elohim and Yahweh. As you remember, Elohim, which means Creator, is the name of God linked with general revelation (Gen. 1—2), and Yahweh (LORD) is His personal, experiential, and salvific name, which characterizes His special revelation (Gen. 2:4; Ex. 3:14–15).

| **Who He is** | **What He is Doing** |
|---|---|
| Elohim | Work of Creation |
| Yahweh | Work of Redemption/Salvation |

Now, with these categories established, let's determine *how* He works in both creation and redemption. Do you see who the driving force behind all creation and redemption is? It has been His plan from eternity past. In fact, the statement that "God the Father has the Plan (will), through His beloved Son, by the power of His Spirit" is the driving force behind everything in His creation, every book of God's Word, and every life ever created.

Therefore, to clearly see this statement played out in Scripture, let's start by looking at who He is and what He is doing in creation. Pay close attention to how he accomplishes His plan.

**Creation**

Genesis 1:1–3a states, "In the beginning, God (Elohim) created the heavens and the earth. And the earth was formless and void, and darkness was over the surface of the deep, and the Spirit of God was moving over the waters. And God said..."

**Note:** The terms "formless and void" can be translated chaos and disorder.

1. Look at the following cross-references to help us understand. In the space provided, note who the subject is, what He is called, and what He is doing.

a. John 1:1–3 –

b. Colossians 1:15–17 (you may need to start at verse 13 because the pronouns can be confusing at times.)

Now, re-read Genesis 1:1–3a: Can you see the Father's Plan (Will)

Do you see the Spirit of God moving?

Do you see through Whom the creation of the world is occurring?

Picture it in this way:

In summary, we understand that God's plan in His work of creation was accomplished *by* the power of His Spirit *through* His Son, the Word. In fact, we know that He spoke, and "it was so" (Gen. 1:3, 6, 9, 11, 14, 20, 24, and 26; Ex. 20:11; Ps. 33:6, 9; 90:2; Isa. 40:26; 45:18; 48:13; Jn. 1:3; Acts 14:15; Rom. 4:17; 1 Cor. 8:6; Col. 1:16; Heb. 11:3; and Rev. 4:11).

We know, following the world's creation, the first catastrophic event recorded on earth occurred—the Fall of Mankind (Genesis 3:1–14), leaving Adam and Eve (and all of humanity afterward) in spiritual chaos, disorder, and darkness. Did you notice the emphasis on the earth? That's because there was a heavenly revolt before the devastating rebellion on earth (see Isaiah 14 and Ezekiel 28 for more details). So, is our sovereign God caught off guard by either? Not if He is truly sovereign, and we know that He is. We know because He tells us in Genesis 3:15 immediately following the Fall and before the curse was put on mankind and the earth. In other words, God the Father has had a plan.

**The Promise of Redemption**

You will recall from a previous lesson, in Genesis 3:15, the LORD God said to the serpent, "I will put enmity between you and the woman, between your seed and her seed; He shall bruise you on the head, and you shall bruise Him on the heel." In other words, it's as if the LORD God is saying, "Here's My plan from eternity past—My eternal plan, which will not be thwarted because I am God and there is no other" (see Isa. 45:5). My eternal plan will not end in bad news, instead, I have good news—the promise of the gospel of Jesus Christ. We know that the Father's plan from eternity past would be accomplished *through* His Son, who would ultimately and victoriously crush the head of the serpent *by* the power of His Spirit.

Do you see it in Genesis 3:15?

Now, before we proceed, we need to gather a little more information as we have paused to do in previous lessons, which will be helpful from this point forward. We need to understand the concept of biblical typology.

In its simplest definition, a "type" is a picture in the Old Testament of a New Testament truth (or antitype). Some refer to a type as a "shadow," and the "substance" would represent the antitype or New Testament counterpart.

Whatever you may choose to describe it, remember that nothing and no one can provide a perfect representation since nothing can adequately describe the "antitype" or "substance," which is Christ.

According to the *Evangelical Dictionary of Theology*, the word "type" comes from the Greek word for "form" or "pattern," and there are several categories—persons, (like Adam or Moses), events (such as the Flood or the brazen serpent), institutions (like the feasts), places, (Jerusalem, Zion, etc.), objects (such as the altar of burnt offering, incense), offices (*eg*., prophet, priest, and king) that can represent a type.[1]

Given this information, let's proceed.

**The Redemption of Israel**

Continuing in Scripture, as time passed, the Father's plan to redeem became even more visible as He revealed His name, LORD, which He explained through His work in the redemption of Israel from Pharaoh when they were held captive in Egypt (Ex. 3).

With the "type" and "antitype" in mind, let's think through Israel's deliverance. You will recall, we saw His redemptive plan for Israel in the first lesson, when the name LORD was introduced and defined by God Himself (Exodus 3:1–15). We learned His redemptive name, LORD, was personal, experiential, and leading to salvation as He Himself rescued His people. But we didn't look at the "types" in the story and what each represents.

For example,

- Pharaoh is a "type" who represents Satan. He is called "the god of this world" (2 Cor. 4:4).
- Egypt is a picture or "type" of the world.
- Israel's slavery is a picture of our bondage to sin.
- Moses is a "type" of Christ who will be the instrument the Father uses to set His people free.

With these things in mind, do you see the picture of redemption associated with the name, LORD?

God the Father sovereignly and purposefully acted (providence). Scripture states, He "came down to deliver" His people (Ex. 3:8). He had "seen their affliction, and given heed to their cry, and was aware of their sufferings" (Ex. 3:7). And then, He introduced Himself to Moses as the "I AM," the LORD.

Can you see the Father's plan to save would be accomplished *through* His Son, *by* the power of His Spirit as Moses spoke God's Word to Pharoah? Moses was just the human instrument the LORD used to deliver His people. The LORD was the true deliverer.

Are you beginning to see the pattern?

1 Walter A. Elwell, Ed., *Evangelical Dictionary of Theology*, 2nd Ed., (Grand Rapids, MI.: Baker Academic) 1222.

God the Father accomplished His Plan (His Will) In the chaos, disorder, and darkness

***Through*** His beloved Son, of Israel's situation.

***By*** the power of His Spirit (who uses His Word)

Now, let's fast-forward in Scripture and place the Book of Ruth in the progression of stories from Scripture. (Keep in mind, every story before and after Ruth's story fits into the same picture.)

Let's recap the highlights of things we have seen using the split screen we used as we studied the Book of Ruth. We will begin our review with Chapter One.

Look at the visual/chart provided and answer the questions that follow.

Chapter One

| Providence | Depravity, Judgment/Mercy |
|---|---|
| "Now it came about (v. 1a) | ...in the days when the judges governed, |
| | that there was a famine in the land. |
| | Elimelech, Naomi, Mahlon, and Chilion |
| | leave Bethlehem "House of Bread" |
| | and |
| | go to Moab (vv. 1b–2) |
| | Death, marriage, and more death enter (vv. 3–5). |
| Naomi "heard" the LORD had visited His people (v. 6) | |
| | Key repeated word: Return (Heb., *sub*): (used 12x) |
| | Naomi returns, and Ruth turns: |
| | To God |
| | To His people |
| | To the "House of Bread" (vv. 6–16) |
| | Orpah walks for a time and then returns to Moab (vv. 14–15) |

1. As you read how Naomi "heard" what the LORD was doing and that she returned, what do you see about the LORD and His providence? In other words, do you think Naomi woke up one day and randomly "heard," and then she chose all on her own to repent? (To help answer, you may need to look at 2 Tim. 2:25b, along with Acts 5:31, Rom. 2:4, and 2 Pet. 3:9.)

Could her ability to hear be a result of God's Spirit and God's Word at work?

2. Now, re-read Ruth 1:20b–21 and answer the following questions:

a. From Naomi's perspective, what does she state, and what name of God does she use?

". . . the ___________________ has ____________________________________ (v. 20).

b. I went out ___________ but the _____________ has _________________

_______ ____________ _____________" (v. 21).

c. Do you see it? What did the Lord (His personal, experiential, and saving name) do for Naomi?

Notice she did not say, "I came back when I just happened to hear that there was bread." She knows who brought her back, and we know it was not just for physical bread, right?

d. Look at her questions to the women in verse 21 again. What is she acknowledging about God in her questions? _____________________________________________

Notice she recognizes the discipline of the LORD, and although she can see His providence in her life, she has yet to recognize His grace. That is, until the LORD begins to open her eyes in chapters 2–4.

**Personal Thoughts**

Did you notice the change of subjects in verse 21? Naomi states, "I went out full," but "the LORD has brought me back." The LORD—His saving name (Ex. 3:8–14). The name that embodies "He who began a good work in us will complete it" (Phil. 1:6). She went out—out from God's people, away from God's promised land, away from where His presence dwelt. But the LORD—praise God for the BUT God portions in Scripture! Isn't that what the LORD does for us?

And although from Naomi's perspective, she is "empty," from God's perspective, right next to her stands Ruth. Unbeknownst to Naomi, she will be the instrument God uses in the good and complete work of His precious and providential care—not only for Naomi but all of Israel's and our future hope as well.

In fact, Naomi's assessment of her situation makes me think of what the LORD says He is doing when He sends out His Word through Jeremiah, His prophet in Jeremiah 1:10. Look at this verse and note the order. Do you see the similarity? Did you catch the end result of "build and to plant?" Did you notice what must happen before His Word "builds and plants"? First, He must empty us. And no one wants that, right?

Moreover, Naomi's use and the Spirit's record of the names of God is not accidental. Think back to the Scripture's first use when the LORD God declares to Abram, "I am God Almighty" (Gen. 17:1). Here, God inaugurates His covenant with Abram, changing his name to Abraham who would be "the father of a multitude of nations" (Gen. 17:5). In other words, the promise of the "seed" would be none other than by the Almighty who can take a woman (Sarah), who is past the age of childbearing, and an old man (Abraham) and bring life into their very barren and seemingly dead situation. In other words, impossible situation—powerful God!

Similarly, the name LORD, His personal covenant name, in which He promises salvation, is equally fitting for the context in which Naomi finds herself, except the whole story has yet to unfold.

3. So, before we proceed in our review to Ruth 2—4, let's recap:

Whose plan do you see in the opening words and in verses 20–21? ______________________

*By* the power of whom and what in verse 6? ________________ using the _______________

Keep that in mind as we progress through the story.

Next, in the narrative, we were introduced to a man at the beginning of Chapter 2, who, as we quickly discovered, became a vital and pivotal character in the story. In fact, he became the primary focus as he changed the entire outcome for Elimelech, Naomi, Ruth, and generations to come.

So, let's focus our full attention on the right side of the screen as we focus in on one man to recap who he is, what he savs. and what he does in chapters two-four, for these things will cause us to see Another.

I. Who enters the story and changes everything? ____________ (2:1)

From what tribe of Israel does he belong (compare 2:1 with 1:2).

II. Next, record where he is from? ____________________ (1:2)

Can you think of Another who was from the tribe of Judah and the town of Bethlehem?

III. Now, in keeping with the story, we want to highlight some of the main events from chapters 2–4, but this time, allow me to provide you with a list of facts we have discovered in previous lessons.

Boaz:

- Is a kinsman of Naomi's husband (2:1)
- Is described as a man of great wealth (strength) (2:1)
- Is obedient to the Word (specifically Lev.25:47–49 and Deut. 25:5–6)
- Takes care of the widow and the foreigner (Ruth 2)
- Gives grace to Ruth (2:10, 13)

- Invites Ruth to a place in the field and at his table (among the Israelite maids) (2:8, 14)
- Serves Ruth from his table (2:14)
- Is lavish in provision (2:15–16)
- Satisfies the hunger in Ruth and Naomi (2:14, 18)
- Serves as a protector to Ruth (2:9, 21–22; 3:14)
- Is filled with *hesed* and can identify it in others (2:13, 20)
- Becomes the security and rest for Naomi and Ruth (3:1, 18)
- Is a keeper of the Law (3:11–12; 4:1–2)
- Fulfills the three requirements of kinsman redeemer from the Word (Deut. 25:5–6; Ruth 4:4, 9–10)
- Is a close relative
- Has the power and is able to redeem
- Is willing to redeem
- Fulfills the role of kinsman-redeemer in the name of the dead to ensure the family of the deceased a future inheritance (4:5–6)
- Takes a Gentile bride to himself (4:13)
- Takes his place in the lineage of King David (4:17, 22)
- Takes his place in the line of the King of kings (Matt. 1:5–6, 16)

Quite the list, wouldn't you say?

**Putting the Pieces Together**
As we proceed, remember, the puzzle we are putting together now will represent the previous, underlying, and much bigger story of redemption from before the foundation of the world. Of all the people we encountered in the book of Ruth, we discovered Boaz was the most obvious "type" of Christ (the antitype).

I. Let's look at the Person of Christ and what qualifies Him to be called the closest kinsman-redeemer. (Note: The verses listed are by no means exhaustive. There are so many more places in Scripture that can be referenced. But for the sake of brevity, I will list only a few.)

a. Read John 1:1–2; Colossians 1:15–16; Hebrews 1:2–3, and 1 Peter 1:20 and record what you see regarding Jesus Christ's identity. He is ___________________________

b. Now, look at Luke 1:31–32, 35 and John 1:14. What do you see about Jesus Christ?

He became _______________________

**Note:** Theologians refer to the fact that Jesus Christ is both God and Man or the God-Man as the hypostatic union, wherein Jesus Christ is 100-percent God and 100-percent man.

Can you see that although He is God, He became man? He never ceased being God, for that is an impossibility. Philippians 2:6–7 explains it this way, stating, Christ Jesus, "who . . . existed in the form of God, did not regard equality with God a thing to be grasped, but *emptied Himself by taking* [emphasis added] the form of a bond-servant, and being made in the likeness of men. . . ."

Do you see how He emptied Himself? The answer is in the text. He did so "by taking the form of a bond-servant." Comments by New Testament scholar and professor, Bruce Ware will be most helpful here as he explains,

> "Christ poured Himself out, taking the form of a servant. Yes, He pours out by taking; He empties by adding. Here, then, is a strange sort of math that envisions a subtraction by addition, an emptying by adding. What can this mean? In brief, what this must mean is this: Christ Jesus, existing and remaining fully who He is as God, accepts His divine calling to come to earth and *carry out the mission assigned Him by the Father*" (emphasis mine).1

You see, from the eternal counsel of the Godhead: God the Father has a plan (will) to save, *through* the Son, *by* the power of His Spirit (emphasis on the prepositions added). This is the gospel (good news)!

c. Why would the hypostatic union (fully God and fully Man) make Him the perfect and only redeemer for mankind?

Think about it; as God, He cannot die, for as God, it would be impossible to die. Therefore, for God to complete His work of redemption, it would be necessary for Him to become a man to redeem His people from their sins. Only God can completely satisfy the demands and holiness of God. And because He is the sinless man, He is the perfect substitute for sinful man.

II. Now, let's look at the significance of places concerning our Redeemer.

a. Read John 6:38, 41, 48, and 51. From where did He originally come?

b. Read Micah 5:2 and Matthew 2:1. Where did the Man, Christ Jesus' story begin? ________________________

c. What about the significance of Bethlehem, "House of Bread"? Any correlation with Christ specifically in terms of redemption? Read John 6:29–40 and record your insights. (Note: The context is right after the miraculous feeding of the 5,000 (+) in John 6:1–14).

III. In this next section, we will look one by one at the events listed earlier in the lesson concerning Boaz as a "type." You should see some clear correlations with Christ. Under each fact in which Boaz serves as a type,

1 *Ibid.*, 20.

record how Jesus Christ serves as the "antitype."

1. Boaz

•Is a kinsman of Naomi's husband (2:1).

Jesus Christ

We have already noted John 1:1–2, 14 and Philippians 2:6–7 prove His identity as both God and man. In this section, we want to further emphasize His identify as the perfect "kinsman" for both God and humanity. In the space provided, record your observations.

a. Matthew 1:23 -

b. Romans 1:3–4

c. 1 Timothy 2:5 -

d. Hebrews 2:14–17 -

There are many more places we could have gone. Feel free to add your own references.

2. Boaz

- Is described as a man of great wealth (strength) (2:1).

Jesus Christ

a. Genesis 14:19 – Note what He possess as God. ___________________________

and

___________________________

b. Jeremiah 32:17 – _

**Note:** One attribute that describes God is His omnipotence, which means He is all-powerful. The Omni attributes (omniscience—all-knowledge, omnipresence—all-present) can only be said about God.

c. 2 Corinthians 8:9 - ______________________________________________

______________________________________________________________

3. Boaz

- Is obedient to the Word (specifically Lev.25:47–49 and Deut. 25:5–6).

Jesus Christ

a. John 5:30b - __________________________________________________

b. John 6:38 - ___________________________________________________

c. John 17:4 - ___________________________________________________

d. Matthew 26:36–44 – Record what Jesus asks the Father and concludes three times:

____________________________________________________________

4. Boaz

- Takes care of the widow and the foreigner (Ruth 2).

Jesus Christ

a. Matthew 25:40 (see vv. 35–40 for context)- ____________________________

____________________________________________________________

b. James 1:27 - __________________________________________________

____________________________________________________________

c. Galatians 3:28 – Jesus' death provided for all, for there is no partiality with God (Rom. 2:11). _____________________________________________________

____________________________________________________________

5. Boaz

- Gives grace to Ruth (2:10, 13).

Jesus Christ

a. John 1:14b, 16 - ______________________________________________

b. Ephesians 2:8–9 - _____________________________________________

6.Boaz

- Invited Ruth a place in the field and at his table (among the Israelite maids) (2:8, 14).

Jesus Christ

a. Matthew 26:26–29 – Note who is serving and the symbolism of what they are eating.

b. 1 Corinthians 11:23–26 – Paul teaches the Corinthian believers about the Lord's Table. What do you see? Include who is welcome to partake.

c. Revelation 19:6–9 – Note who is present and why they are described in that way. Include what the celebration is called.

7. Boaz

- Lavish in provision (2:15–16).

Jesus Christ

a. John 10:11, 15 - ____________________________________________________

b. Ephesians 5:2 ______________________________________________________

Is there anything more lavish?

8. Boaz

- Satisfies the hunger in Ruth and Naomi (2:14, 18).

Jesus Christ

a. John 4:14 - ________________________________________________________

b. John 6:35 - ________________________________________________________

9. Boaz

- Serves as a protector to Ruth (2:9, 21–22; 3:14).

Jesus Christ

a. Psalm 23 and John 10 - ____________________________________________

____________________________________________________________

10. Boaz

- Is filled with *hesed* and can identify it in others (2:13, 20).

Jesus Christ

a. Titus 3:4–5 - ____________________________________________________

____________________________________________________________

b. Galatians 5:22–24 - ______________________________________________

11. Boaz

- Becomes the security and rest for Naomi and Ruth (3:1, 18).

Jesus Christ

a. Matthew 11:28–30 ____________________________________________

__________________________________________________________

b. John 14:27 - _____________________________________________________

12. Boaz

- Keeper of the Law (3:11-12; 4:1-2).

Jesus Christ

a. Matthew 5:17–18 - ______________________________________________

13. Boaz

- Fulfills the three requirements of kinsman-redeemer from the Word (Deut. 25:5–6; Ruth 4:4, 9–10).

  Is a close relative

  Has the power and is able to redeem

  Is willing to redeem

Jesus Christ

a. Philippians 2:7–8. If you look closely, you will see what qualifies Him as both Kinsman and Redeemer.

verse 7 ________________________________________________________

verse 8 ________________________________________________________

14. Boaz

- Fulfills the role of kinsman-redeemer in the name of the dead to ensure the family members of the deceased a future inheritance (4:5–6).

Jesus Christ

a. Ephesians 2:1, and 4-7 – Note our condition prior to salvation, and what He did to secure our inheritance. ______________________________________________

_________________________________________________________________

b. 1 Peter 1:2-5 – Can you see the Father, Son, and Spirit?
Record what you learn about our inheritance. ____________________________________________________

_________________________________________________________________

15. Boaz

- Takes a Gentile Bride to himself (4:13).

Jesus Christ

a. Ephesians 2:13–14 - ____________________________________________________

_________________________________________________________________

Again, Revelation 19:6–9 (see above).

16. Boaz

- Takes his place in the lineage of King David (4:17, 22).

Jesus Christ

a. Matthew 1:1 - __________________________________________________

Matthew traces Jesus' line through Solomon, David's son (Matt. 1:6)

b. Luke 3:31 - ____________________________________________________

Luke traces Jesus' line through Nathan, David's son (Lk. 3:31).

17. Boaz

- Takes his place in the line of the King of kings (Matt. 1:5–6, 16).

Jesus Christ

a. Revelation 19:16 - __________________________________________________

As you consider all these things, don't you find Him absolutely beautiful?

One final picture to consider in the story of Ruth: can you see the alignment?

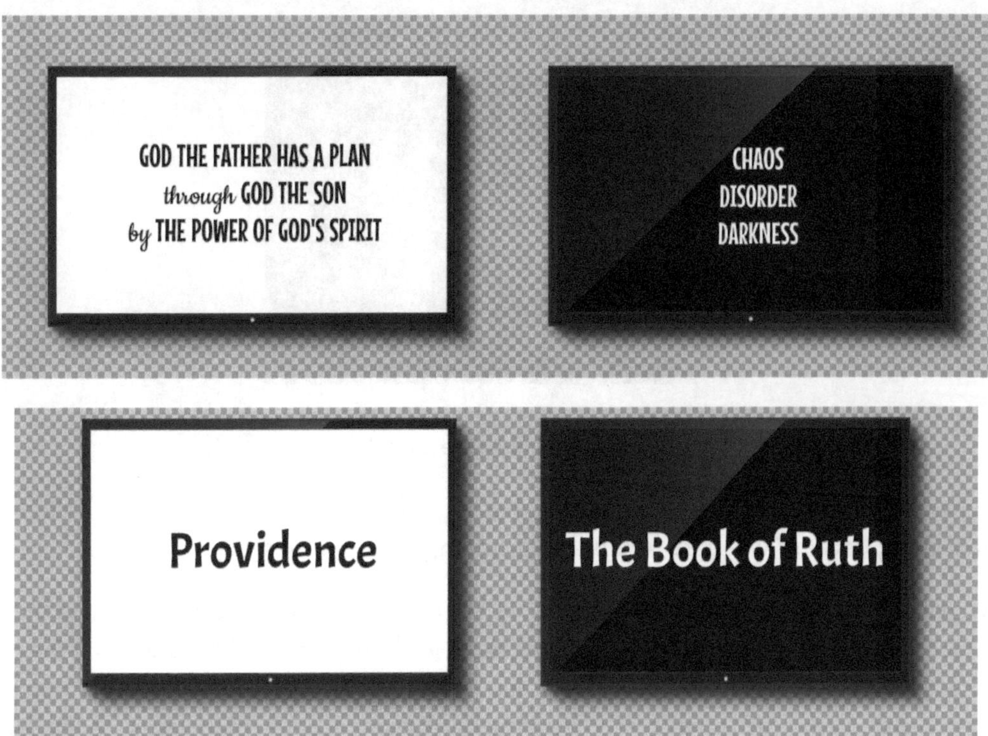


Now, having put together the People, places, and events hidden within the left side of the puzzle, can you see the bigger picture inside the story of Naomi, Ruth, and Boaz? Do you see the picture God's providence was unveiling?

God the Father's Plan (His Will)

***Through*** His beloved Son,

***By*** the power of His Spirit!

God's providence purposefully entered the chaos, disorder, and darkness of one obscure Jewish family's life, bringing peace into the chaos, order out of disorder, and light into the darkness!

Beautiful, isn't He?

Furthermore, as you think about the believers in the Old and New Testament, consider these things:

| <u>Believers in the Old Testament</u> | | <u>Believers in the New Testament</u> |
|---|---|---|
| | Out of Chaos, Disorder, and Darkness | |
| They awaited the promised Messiah. | | We await our Savior's Second Coming. |
| | Out of ordinary, mundane | |
| | Times of economic hardship | |
| | Times of grief and death | |
| They looked forward to their Savior. | | We look back at our Savior. |

Do you see all who are His are looking one place?

Have you looked to Jesus to be saved (Isaiah 45:22)?

In conclusion, typically, it's assumed that every story has an ending. Still, we know that the story is ongoing for Naomi, Ruth, and Boaz, because it is part of God's continuing and eternal story.

And part of what makes the book of Ruth so unique is that His providence has purposed that it is the only book in the Old Testament that ends with the genealogy of a man who humbled himself in obedience to fulfill the role of a kinsman-redeemer that directly picks back up in the New Testament with the genealogy of a Man who humbled Himself and became obedient to death, even death on a cross to become our Kinsman-Redeemer, Jesus Christ (Matthew 1).

And throughout the gospels, the narrative of His life and death is recorded. And though His story, as Man, ends in death, that is not the end of His story because our Kinsman-Redeemer resurrected from the dead, and He is alive forevermore! He is seated at the Father's right hand, and He is coming back; therefore, while the redeemed of the Lord wait, each is compelled to say so! His story is still being told in and through the lives of His redeemed today, and because our Redeemer lives, our story has a happy ending, an eternity with our Kinsman-Redeemer!

Therefore, consequently after studying the Book of Ruth, one might say when the eternal Kinsman-Redeemer on the left side of the screen providentially enters into the depravity of our story on the right because of His great *hesed*, we, like Ruth, were given a place, lavish provision, and protection (justification) and now, like Naomi, find ourselves eternally grateful to the Father who is purposefully emptying us (as needed) in order to fill us as He continues to conform us into the image of His Son (sanctification) as we eagerly await His presence (glorification). So, let the redeemed of the Lord say so!

What's your story?

In the space on the next page, prayerfully ask the Father to reveal His providence in your life as He has saved you through His Son by the power of God's Spirit as He used the Word. Have you taken the time to document it? Who knows, your children or grandchildren may read your story someday. Wouldn't you want them to see His providence in your life as it is part of their stories, too?

As you reflect on your story, do you realize it is actually part of a much bigger story from eternity past? Do you see how God has used all things: the good, dark, and difficult things in your life to bring you to Himself (Rom. 8:28) and how His providence is continually shaping you into the image of His beloved Son (Rom. 8:29)? This profound realization should fill you with hope and great joy, as you witness the transformative power of God's providence in your life. As you write, take the time to thank and praise Him as you go. Your prayer will be a sweet aroma before His throne of grace!

*Hallelujah!*

*What a Savior!*

In closing, I want to share the story of a dear friend in ministry who was asked to give her story at a lady's event. The Scripture, "Let the redeemed say so" (Ps. 107:2), was the assignment. However, after having written her testimony, I noticed that she was very tearful and troubled. When I asked her about it, she shared with me how her dark past was causing a lot of shame and guilt and how fear of others knowing it was a paralyzing thought. As the event approached, I saw a visible peace settle over her. I will never forget what she said when I asked her what had changed. She told how she had poured all her shame, guilt, and fear before the Lord about "her" story and how the Lord, in His perfect lovingkindness, brought to her mind, "This is not your story; it is Mine." Her courage to share "His" story transformed her heart and inspired others to be willing to do the same. So, I encourage you to be willing and ready to share "His" story for His glory. I promise He will use it to result in your good.

Hopefully, the Father's plan through His Son by the power of God's Spirit, who uses His Word is what you and others will see as you share "your" story, for as Scripture clearly states, "Salvation belongs to the LORD" (Ps. 3:8; Ps. 62:1, Jonah 2:9, and Rev. 7:10; 19:1).

# The Book of Ruth

## Appendix

### LESSON ONE

**The Providence of God**

I realize tracing the providence of God is a rather extensive work since everything He does is purposeful. However, I have provided some of the highlights of His providential work in the Pentateuch from Genesis to the time of Ruth (the Judges) to allow you to see what they knew and had access to. Remember, these examples are not meant to be exhaustive but informative. Many more things could have been included under the topic, the Providence of God.

You will recall in the lesson, we looked at God's Providence in His purposeful work of Creation and Redemption. Let's continue where we left off in the book of Genesis. Remember, you are looking for and only recording God's Purposeful acts.

As we continue to read the Pentateuch, watch as you see the same pattern throughout the Scriptures: God's providence (His purposeful acts) in the work of His redemption runs parallel with man's continually choosing his way and remaining responsible and accountable before God.

**The Flood**

1.. Look at Genesis 6:1-8, and answer the following questions:

a. What is the first phrase in verse 1? ______________________________________

Did you catch the phrase "Now it came about... (v. 1)"? When thinking about the providence of God in Scripture, you will typically see phrases like this to introduce a somewhat hidden yet salvific work of God.

b. Now, read Genesis 6:2-7. In this part of history's narrative, we are told in verse 2, that "the sons of God saw that the daughters of men were beautiful; and they took wives for themselves, whoever they chose."

**Note:** I realize that this verse is very difficult to understand, please allow me to explain. The term, "sons of God" (*bene Elohim*) is a reference to angels (see Job 1:6). We are told more about these angels in Jude 6, which states, "And angels who did not keep their own domain, but abandoned their proper abode, He has kept in eternal bonds under darkness for the judgment of the great day."

You see, by not keeping their domain, and abandoning their proper abode (as angels), these fallen angels took wives among the domain and abode of humanity. Their union produced "mighty men who were of old, men of renown (v. 4).

c. Notice what the Scriptures record next in verse 5?

Both the fallen angels and humanity would be severely punished. These fallen angels were placed in "eternal bonds," awaiting God's final judgment. Humanity, however, would be wiped off the face of the earth in a judgment of God known as the Flood, except for the grace of God toward one man and his family.

d. Read and record Genesis 6:8. What do you see?

**Note:** In Luke 8: 26–39, when Jesus casts out demons from the man who lived among the tombs in the country of the Gerasenes (vv. 26–27). Immediately the demons recognized who Jesus was and asked, "What do I have to do with YOU, Jesus, Son of the Most High God? I beg You, do not torment me" (v. 28). When Jesus asked their name, they answered, "Legion"; for many demons had entered him" (v. 30). Then they begged Him not to command them to depart to the abyss (v. 31).

Interestingly, the demons knew about the "abyss" in which the demons from Genesis 6 were being kept.

**The Tower of Babel**

2. Now, look at Genesis 11:2.

a. What phrase introduces the purposeful action of God?

b. As you read Genesis 11:2-9, how and from what is the providence of God saving humanity? Be sure to include what man is doing.

**Note:** Phrases like "Come let us build for ourselves" and "let us make ourselves a name" are clear indicators that humanity is turning in rebellion against the LORD (v. 4). Babel represents the first city since the flood to try and thwart God's plan. It is man's determined attempt to build his religious system to get to heaven, defying God's provision of one way.

In His mercy, the LORD came down, and in judgment, He scattered them abroad by confusing their language (v. 8). Again, providence exercised His purposeful acts to save mankind from himself.

**The LORD Calls Abram to Himself**

3. Genesis 12:1–3. In this section, record who calls whom. Record the purposeful actions (providence of God) in this passage. What is God's intent on calling Abram out? [Keep in mind, Abram is a polytheist (a worshiper of many gods) from Ur (Babylon), and he is not looking for God nor knows that God exists.]

**Abram's Day of Salvation**

4. Genesis 15:6, and 12–18a - Record God's purposeful actions (providence) in this passage. What is God's intent on making a covenant, and with whom is He making it?

    a. What is recorded in verse 6?

**The LORD Inaugurates the Covenant with Himself**

    b. Now record facts concerning the covenant the LORD made in verses 12–18a.

Have you caught who is initiating and making the covenant and with whom it is being made? Be careful not to say Abraham because Abraham is in a "deep sleep" (v.12). Essentially, he is the beneficiary of the covenant God is making with Himself, isn't he?

Now record how the LORD establishes His covenant with Abraham.

**The LORD Establishes His Covenant with Abraham**

5. Read Genesis 17:7, 19, 21 – (For context, read Gen. 17:1–21). Record what God is doing in these verses and with whom He intends to do it.

**The LORD Tests Abraham's Faith**

6. Now, read Genesis 22 and Hebrews 11:17–19. How is the providence of God hidden but evident in this chapter? In other words, how is the providence (purposeful acts) of God embedded in this story? Record your insights below.

**Deliverance From Egypt**

7. Read Exodus 2:11 – Record the phrase frequently used to introduce God's providence and with whom He is about to work.

8. Now, look at Exodus 3 and record evidence of the providence of God in His salvific work of redemption. What do you see?

9. Read Exodus 9:16; 14:4, 17–18 and record the purpose of God's providence by allowing the plagues and the hardening of Pharoah's heart as recorded in Scripture.

   a. What do you see regarding God? ________________________________________

   b. What do you see concerning God's people? _________________________________

Did you see that God's providence assures God's glory and man's good?

10. Now, read Exodus 12:1–14. What is the purpose God's providence in this part of the Exodus (v. 13)?

**The Giving of God's Law**

11. Now, read and record the beginning words in Exodus 19:16.

12. Now read Exodus 19:20. How do the words in Exodus 19:16 introduce the LORD'S purposeful actions?

13. Read Exodus 20:2 and record the words of the LORD.

Do you see the connection between God's providence (announced in Ex. 19:16) and the reminder of His work of redemption (Ex. 20:2) when the LORD came down to give Moses the Law (Ex. 19:20)?

In the giving of the Law in reference to providence, John Piper states,

> God saw to it that His ultimate goal in providence was embedded at the center of Israel's written constitution. That goal is that His worth and beauty be magnified above all things in His people's heartfelt worship of His excellence. Or to say it another way, the goal of God's providence, now established at the center of His law, is that He be exalted as the greatest treasure in the glad affections of His people—that He be supremely glorified through our being supremely satisfied in Him.[1]

As we proceed in Scripture, keep in mind that the book of Leviticus covers only one month. (See Exodus 40:17 and compare it with Numbers 1:1.) In the book of Leviticus, the providence of God in His redemptive work is seen in the instruction of the five main offerings: the burnt offering (Lev. 1), the meal offering (Lev. 2), the peace offering (Lev. 3), the sin offering (Lev. 4), and the trespass offering (Lev. 5).

**The Anointing of Aaron as Israel's First High Priest**

14. Read and record the first phrase in Leviticus 9:1.

**Note:** As we have consistently seen, phrases like this can be seen periodically throughout Israel's history, giving evidence to God's often hidden and obscure, yet providential care. And God remains faithful even while Israel consistently responds in unbelief, sin, and rebellion.

If you were to continue to read Leviticus 9, you would discover the providence of God in the anointing of Aaron as Israel's first high priest and his sons to serve before the LORD as priests.

**The Feasts of Israel**

Additionally, Israel was to celebrate nine feasts, all pointing to the providence of God. The first three served to remind Israel of God's creative work, specifically: the weekly Sabbath (Lev. 23:1–3), the seven-year Sabbath feast (Lev. 25:2–7), and the fiftieth year Sabbath (Lev. 25:8–16).

The remaining six feasts represented His redemptive work, namely: the Passover feast (Lev. 23:4–8), the feast of first fruits (Lev. 23: 9–14), the feast of Pentecost (Lev. 23:15–25), the feast of trumpets (Lev. 23:23–25), the Day of Atonement feast (Lev. 23:26–32), and the feast of tabernacles (Lev. 23:33–44).

As Israel's story progresses in Numbers, evidence of God's providence is seen throughout the book, which takes its name from two separate occasions when the LORD instructed a census be taken in (first in Num. 1—2, and the second one thirty-eight years later in Num. 26:2, in the desert of Moab).

**Failure to Enter the Promised Land at Kadesh: Sin of Unbelief**

Tragically, out of the 603,550 males (twenty years of age and older) who were numbered in the first census, not counting the Levites (Num. 2:32–33), only two (Caleb and Joshua) were able to enter the promised land by the second census (Num. 26:2) due to Israel's sin of unbelief (Num. 13—14).

1 Piper, *Providence*, 115.

15. Let's pause here and read Numbers 14. Notice the reaction of the Israelites following the "bad report" from the spies (leaders from each tribe) sent out to scope out the land (Num. 13:32).

a. Briefly summarize their response in verses 1–4.

b. Now, record how Moses, Aaron, Joshua, and Caleb respond in verses 5–9.

c. When "all the congregation said to stone them with stones," who showed up in verse 10?

d. Read verses 11–16 and summarize the conversation between Moses and the LORD.

Now, read verses 17–19. Do you see how Moses appeals to the LORD based on who He is and His providential work of redemption rather than the Israelites who had repeatedly proven to be undeserving of God's mercy?

e. Record the loving-kindness and faithfulness of the LORD in verse 20. What do you see?

f. Now, read the LORD's response regarding the consequences of their actions in verses 21–23. What do you see

Are you beginning to see the evidence of God's providence carefully and consistently interwoven throughout each book?

**Moses' Three Speeches to Israel's Second Wilderness Generation**

Now, let's look at God's providence in Deuteronomy, and allow me to summarize a few of the highlights in the book wherein Moses preaches three sermons, reminding Israel of God's faithfulness (Deut. 2:7; 4:33-38; 7:6–8; 8:3–4; 9:4–6; 29:5–6; 32:9–14), and the importance of God's Word (Deut. 4:1–2, 7, 9; 11:18–21; and 30:11–14).[1] Other topics include the person, love, glory, grace, and the will of God.

1 Harold L. Willmington, *Willmington's Guide to the Bible*, (Wheaton, Il.: Tyndale House Publishers, 1984), 84.

**Blessings and Curses**
In addition, the providence of God is witnessed in the blessings from Mount Gerizim, and the curses from Mount Ebal are read by the Levitical priests "on the day they cross the Jordan" (Deut. 27:9–13).

The blessings are specified in Deuteronomy 28:1–14, while the curses are identified in verses 27:15–26 and Deuteronomy 28:15–68. Make no mistake, throughout the book of Deuteronomy, the children of Israel have been repeatedly warned and providentially reminded of God's work of redemption continually. In other words, they were without excuse.

**Joshua Appointed to Lead**
And now, in the progression of Israel's history, we find ourselves in the book of Joshua.

16. Begin by reading and recording Joshua 1:1.

17. Now, record the words of God's providence as seen in His redemptive work in Joshua 1:2–5. Summarize the *purposeful actions* (providence) of the LORD as well as His instructions to Joshua.

18. Summarize the providence of God in His work of redemption in Joshua 2, specifically in the life of a harlot from Jericho named Rahab. Record your insights below, especially her words in verses 9–11. What do you see in her?

You may be curious as to why we paused here in Joshua. Would it surprise you to discover that Rahab is the mother of Boaz from our story in Ruth (see Matthew 1:5)?

If you were to read the entire book of Joshua, you would discover the testimony of God's providence through a series of conquests as Israel is given the land of Canaan and witness the work of the LORD as He makes good on His covenant promises to Abraham, Isaac, and Jacob. Most assuredly, the providence of God in his work of redemption is evident as Israel victoriously takes possession of the land.

For now, we will pause here in Israel's history, as we continue to trace the providence of God in the Book of Judges in our next lesson. In fact, an entire lesson will be devoted to the Book of Judges. "Why?" you may ask. The answer is that the first sentence of Ruth requires it.

## LESSON SIX

**Characteristics of a Type**
In a more technical sense, Old Testament theologian and scholar, G.K. Beale has identified five characteristics necessary for something or someone to be considered a type, namely:

Close analogical correspondence of truths about people, events, or institutions. In other words, comparing two different things that are similar.

Historicity

A pointing-forwardness (or what we have termed in our study, a complete/canonical context).

Escalation, wherein the antitype (N.T. correspondence) in some way relates.

Retrospection, which means the idea that it was after Christ's resurrection and under the direction of the Spirit that the apostolic writers understood certain OT historical narratives about persons, events, or institutions to be indirect prophecies of Christ or the church.[1]

**Additional Scriptural Support of our Kinsman-Redeemer**

Now, let's approach redemption from another angle—the purchasing payment and benefit of the recipient. You see, a price had to be paid in order to fulfill the role of the redeemer. As you look at the following cross-references, record the debt that was paid, who paid the debt, what the payment was, and how it is described in the cross-references given. You might discover some overlap with the previous question, but that's okay, right? Record your insights in the space provided.

a. Isaiah 43:1 -

b. Isaiah 52:3 -

c. Matthew 26:28 -

d. John 1:29 – Note the name He is called and what that implies.

e. Acts 20:28 -

1 G. K. Beale, *Handbook on the New Testament Use of the Old Testament: Exegesis and Interpretation* (Grand Rapids, MI.: Baker Academic, 2012), 19.

f. Romans 3:24–26

g. Romans 5:9 –

h. 1 Corinthians 6:19b-20 –

i. 1 Cor. 7:23 –

j. Galatians 2:20-

k. Galatians 3:13 –

l. Galatians 4:4–5 –

m. Ephesians 1:7 -

n. Ephesians 2:13, 16 -

o. Colossians 1:14, 20 -

p. Titus 2:14 -

q. Hebrews 2:14 -

r. Hebrews 9:12, 14, and 22 -

s. Hebrews 10:10, 19–20 -

t. Hebrews 13:12, 20 -

u. 1 Peter 1:18-20 -

v. 1 John 1:7 -

w. 1 John 2:2 -

x. Revelation 1:5 -

y. Revelation 5:9

z. Revelation 7:14–15 -

aa. Revelation 12:11 –

In closing, our final assignment will be in keeping with the praise, glory, and honor our holy, righteous, and faithful Lord is due. You see, according to Scripture, there is one more thing the redeemed of the Lord can, needs to, and must do. Look at Psalm 107 to discover what that is.

Answer the following questions from Psalm 107:

a. What are we told about the LORD in verse 1? 1) ____________________________

2) ____________________________

Would it surprise you that "steadfast love" is translated from the Hebrew word *hesed*?

3) What should our response be ( v.1)?________________________

b. What would you think if I told you that *hesed* serves as a bookend for this entire psalm? Look at the last verse in the psalm (v. 43). What do you see?

c. Now, read verse 2 and record who the psalmist addresses and what they can, need to, and must do as a result: 1) Who? ______________________________

2) What should they do? __________________________

3) From what have they been redeemed? ____________

**Note:** The word "trouble" (*sar*) is a "noun indicating narrowness, tightness, distress, and misery. It is used figuratively of a person's pain and distress; oppression, a feeling of being hemmed in, afflicted, suffering. It can also be used to indicate "an enemy, foe, and adversary, an oppressor."[1]

1 Baker and Carpenter, *The Complete Word Study Dictionary Old Testament*, pp. 966-967.

Think about the believer's three enemies listed in Ephesians 2:2–3 and our final enemy, death (1 Cor. 15:26).

d. Now, let's acknowledge from where the redeemed have been gathered (v. 3)?

1) ___________________________

2) ___________________________

3) ___________________________

4) ___________________________

Does that remind you of Revelation 5:9?

Would that include Ruth, the Moabitess? Does it include you? Aren't you thankful?

e. From verses 4–32, you should see four distinct groups of people and various situations. The groups are divided by the distinction "Some." See if you can find the divisions and form an outline. It may be tempting to look at a commentary or listen to a podcast but try to refrain from doing so. Allow God's Spirit to take His Word and teach you. What do you see?

f. Now, let's conclude the psalm in verses 33–42. Record your insights in this portion of the psalm. What do you see?

And now, fittingly, in light of the study of Ruth, our Kinsman-Redeemer, Jesus Christ, and Psalm 107, would you, the redeemed of the LORD, be willing to say so if given the opportunity? With whom in the book of Ruth do you identify most, and how has your Kinsman-Redeemer used this little Book of Ruth to redeem your soul?